SCIENCE FICTION

Science Fiction is a fascinating and comprehensive introduction to one of the most popular areas of modern culture. This second edition reflects how the field is rapidly changing in both its practice and its critical reception. With an entirely new conclusion and every other chapter fully reworked and updated, this volume:

- offers a concise history of science fiction and the ways in which the genre has been used and defined
- provides explanations of key concepts in SF criticism and theory through chapters that discuss gender, race, technology and metaphor
- examines the interactions between science fiction and science fact
- anchors each chapter with a case study drawn from a short story, book or film, from Frank Herbert's *Dune* to *Star Wars*, from *The Left Hand of Darkness* to *Neuromancer*

Introducing the reader to nineteenth-century, Pulp, Golden Age, New Wave, feminist and cyberpunk science fictions, this is the essential contemporary guide to a major cultural movement.

Adam Roberts is Professor of Nineteenth-Century Literature at Royal Holloway, University of London. He has published many books and articles on nineteenth-century literature and science fiction. His SF novels include *Salt* (2000), *On* (2001) and *Gradisil* (2006).

THE NEW CRITICAL IDIOM

SERIES EDITOR: JOHN DRAKAKIS, UNIVERSITY OF STIRLING

The New Critical Idiom is an invaluable series of introductory guides to today's critical terminology. Each book:

- provides a handy, explanatory guide to the use (and abuse) of the term
- offers an original and distinctive overview by a leading literary and cultural critic
- relates the term to the larger field of cultural representation.

With a strong emphasis on clarity, lively debate and the widest possible breadth of examples, The New Critical Idiom is an indispensable approach to key topics in literary studies.

Also available in this series:

SCIENCE FICTION

Second Edition

Adam Roberts

Routledge
Taylor & Francis Group

LONDON AND NEW YORK

First published 2006
by Routledge
2 Park Square, Milton Park, Abingdon, Oxon OX14 4RN

Simultaneously published in the USA and Canada
by Routledge
711 Third Avenue, New York, NY 10017

Routledge is an imprint of the Taylor & Francis Group, an informa business

© 2006 Adam Roberts

Typeset in Garamond and ScalaSans by
Taylor & Francis Books
Printed and bound in Great Britain by
CPI Antony Rowe, Chippenham, Wiltshire

British Library Cataloguing in Publication Data
A catalogue record for this book is available from the British Library

Library of Congress Cataloging in Publication Data
A catalog record for this book has been requested

ISBN10 0–415–36667–4   ISBN13 978-0-415-36667-4 (hbk)
ISBN10 0–415–36668–2   ISBN13 978-0-415-36668-7 (pbk)

T&F informa

Taylor & Francis Group is the Academic Division of T&F Informa plc.

Contents

SERIES EDITOR'S PREFACE

The New Critical Idiom is a series of introductory books which seeks to extend the lexicon of literary terms, in order to address the radical changes which have taken place in the study of literature during the last decades of the twentieth century. The aim is to provide clear, well-illustrated accounts of the full range of terminology currently in use, and to evolve histories of its changing usage.

The current state of the discipline of literary studies is one where there is considerable debate concerning basic questions of terminology. This involves, among other things, the boundaries which distinguish the literary from the non-literary; the position of literature within the larger sphere of culture; the relationship between literatures of different cultures; and questions concerning the relation of literary to other cultural forms within the context of interdisciplinary studies.

It is clear that the field of literary criticism and theory is a dynamic and heterogeneous one. The present need is for individual volumes on terms which combine clarity of exposition with an adventurousness of perspective and a breadth of application. Each volume will contain as part of its apparatus some indication of the direction in which the definition of particular terms is likely to move, as well as expanding the disciplinary boundaries within which some of these terms have been traditionally contained. This will involve some re-situation of terms within the larger field of cultural representation, and will introduce examples from the area of film and the modern media in addition to examples from a variety of literary texts.

Preface to the Second Edition and Acknowledgements

This second edition of the Routledge New Critical Idiom Science Fiction has been very thoroughly reworked. Several chapters have been extensively rewritten from the first edition, and the final chapter is wholly new, whilst a fair proportion of the first edition has been excised entirely. This reflects two main facts. One is that SF as a field is rapidly developing; its current practice and the body of critical assumptions about its past have changed in the five years since the first edition was issued. The second is that, whilst no book of criticism can hope to be entirely error free, the first edition of this book contained more errors than were acceptable; I am very grateful to the readers and reviewers who pointed out errors. I would like, in particular, to thank Mark Bould, Ria Cheyne, Robert Eaglestone, Malcolm Edwards, Brian Green, Julie Green, Gareth Griffiths, David Langford, Roger Levy, James Lovegrove, Roger Luckhurst, Nick Lowe, Abraham Kawa, Liam McNamara, Una O'Farrell Tate, Gillian Redfern, Rachel Roberts and Simon Spanton. John Drakakis read the entire manuscript and made many helpful suggestions; he has been an exemplary general editor.

1

DEFINING SCIENCE FICTION

The term 'science fiction' resists easy definition. This is a strange thing, because most people have a sense of what science fiction is. Any bookstore will have a section devoted to SF: shelves of mostly brightly coloured paperback volumes, illustrated on their covers with photorealist paintings of intricate spaceships perhaps, or of men and women in futuristic cities or bizarre alien landscapes. Most of these novels are narratives that elaborate some imaginative or fantastic premise, perhaps involving a postulated future society, encounters with creatures from another world, travel between planets or in time. In other words, science fiction as a genre or division of literature distinguishes its fictional worlds to one degree or another from the world in which we actually live: a fiction of the imagination rather than observed reality, a fantastic literature.

But when it comes down to specifying in precisely what ways SF is distinctive, and in what ways it is different from other imaginative and fantastic literatures, there is disagreement. All of the many definitions offered by critics have been contradicted or modified by other critics, and it is always possible to point to texts consensually called SF that fall outside the usual definitions. It is, perhaps, for this reason that some critics try to content themselves with definitions of the mode that are mere tautologies, as if 'we' all know what it is and elaboration is superfluous. Edward James suggests that 'SF is what is marketed as SF' (although he concedes that, as a definition, this is 'a beginning, nothing more') (James 1994: 3). Damon Knight says that 'science fiction is what we point to when we say it'; and Norman Spinraid argues that 'science fiction is anything published as science fiction' (quoted in Clute and Nicholls 1993: 314). There is a kind of weariness in this sort of circular reasoning, as if the whole business of definition is nothing more than a cynical marketing exercise. Lance Parkin suggests that 'SF is a notoriously difficult term to define, but when it comes down to it, a book appears on the SF shelves if the publisher thinks they will maximize their sales by labelling it as such' (Parkin 1999: 4). This mistrust of definition has interesting implications for the self-image of SF as a genre, although it doesn't get us very far as a starting point.

There are different ways of coming at the business of 'definition' of a cultural phenomenon, or collection of texts, such as science fiction. This study attempts to approach the matter from a variety of different perspectives. The danger in this approach is that it may result in an account of SF that is merely fragmented; but its overwhelming advantage is that it does not propose, tacitly or otherwise, that any one approach to this complex matter is the only way. Definitions of SF, like histories of SF, are manifold not because critics and historians of the form are confused, or can't agree on key points, but because SF itself is a wide-ranging, multivalent and endlessly cross-fertilising cultural idiom.

So, one approach to the business of defining SF is to attempt to encapsulate the fundamental conceptual premise or premises out of which science fiction is produced. A related approach is what we might call formalist: the attempt to draw out, from a wide range of specific examples of SF (novels, stories, films and so on), the underlying grammar or essence that they all share. This approach to the business of defining, and indeed describing, SF has been very influential in various critical discourses, and this first chapter, the one you are reading now, will provide key examples of this.

A second approach at definition is what we might call 'historicist'. This seeks to arrive at a definition of the genre not by boiling it down to apothegmic 'rules' or descriptors, but by providing an account of the history of the genre, paying attention to its cultural contexts and effects. Damien Broderick, one of the most insightful current critics of SF, has explored what he calls the 'megatext' of SF, the conglomeration of all those SF novels, stories, films, TV shows, comics and other media with which 'SF fandom' is familiar. The protocols of SF are in large part determined by a knowledge of this 'megatext', and many SF fans are extremely well versed in it. This means that a new SF text – say a new novel set in a world in which Hitler won the Second World War (which is to say an 'alternate history') – will be read by fans who are familiar with some or all of the many previous SF treatments of this theme. Derivative, unoriginal or obtuse treatments will get short shrift. Writers ignorant of the megatext run the risk of in effect reinventing the wheel, or proposing imaginative conceits they consider new and exciting but which have in fact been worked through many times by previous SF writers. Having a sense of the SF megatext is in itself a way of approaching a definition of SF; and this study, by sketching out a number of chronological 'histories of SF' in Chapters 2 and 3, will work in that direction.

According to Roger Luckhurst, in the best of the recent critical accounts of SF, 'a historicist definition of SF necessarily produces a broader, more inclusive definition of SF than a formalist or conceptual one' (Luckhurst 2005: 11). This present study shares this belief to the extent that it is probably true that only somebody with some sense of the history of the genre is in a position to move towards anything as difficult as 'definition'. But the problem here is that there are very many different histories of the genre, sometimes telling stories about SF at odds with one another. One history might see SF as a predominantly male, adolescent, machine-oriented type of writing; another as a mode through which groups who have often been socially marginalised can find imaginative expression, as, for instance, with the many writers and readers of the genre who see it as a way of interrogating questions of gender (this is discussed in Chapter 4), or who see SF's continuing fascination with the alien as a means of exploring issues of race (Chapter 5). Another history would be interested less in the content of SF texts than in the form – not so much the aliens in the story, as the textual strategies of alienation or metaphorisation (Chapter 6).

SOME FORMALIST DEFINITIONS OF SF

The *Oxford English Dictionary* defines science fiction as 'imaginative fiction based on postulated scientific discoveries or spectacular environmental changes, frequently set in the future or on other planets and involving space or time travel', adding that the term did not come into common usage until the 1920s. The terms of this basic dictionary definition are instructive: 'imaginative fiction' differentiates SF from 'realist' fiction, in which there is some attempt at a literary verisimilitude that reproduces the experience of living in the world we recognise as ours. Where the realist writer needs to focus on accuracy, the SF author can use her imagination to invent things not found in our world. These points of difference, the 'scientific discoveries' or 'environmental changes' of the dictionary definition, may be such things as 'space or time travel' but they could be many other premises not listed by the OED, to do with robots, computers, alternative histories and the like. This makes SF a literature of ideas predicated on some substantive difference or differences between the world described and the world in which readers actually live.

But whilst SF is imaginative fiction, it does not follow that all imaginative fiction can be usefully categorised as SF. Stories in which the protagonists travel from Earth to colonies on Mars by rocket ship are usually taken to be science fiction because no such colonies, and no such available mode of transport, are available to us today. But fairytales, surreal fictions (such as André Breton's *Nadja*, 1928) or magic realism (like Salman Rushdie's *Midnight's Children*, 1981) all involve substantive differences between the world of the text and the world the readership actually lives in, and they are not categorised as science fiction. For example, there is a novel by Ian Watson called *The Jonah Kit* (1975), which involves a new technology that maps the brainwave patterns of a human on to the mind of a whale. This human consciousness then inhabits the whale. We might compare this tale with Franz Kafka's short novel *Metamorphosis* (1915), in which the protagonist wakes up one morning to find himself transformed into the shape of a giant insect. Watson's novel is classified as SF, where Kafka's is not. Why should this be? Both are imaginative fictions based on the premise of a radical change; neither is concerned with space or time travel, or is set on other planets. What makes them different?

There could be two answers to this question. The first would assert that science fiction is a much broader category than is usually admitted and should be used to describe a wide range of 'fantasy' literatures; according to this argument, Kafka's *Metamorphosis* is indeed a science-fiction tale, even if it is not usually categorised as such. The second answer would deny this and stress the differences of approach of the two writers. Kafka never explains how his hero turns into a bug: the metamorphosis is literally inexplicable, a physical impossibility. Indeed, Kafka isn't interested in the change as such, which is why he does not feel any need to explain how it has come about. He is interested in the alienation his character subsequently suffers, the reactions of his family to his new monstrosity. In other words, the transformation of man into bug is only a premise, a symbolic facilitator for the subsequent narrative and not a focus for narrative explication in itself. Watson's metamorphosis of man into whale, on the other hand, is placed in a context of scientific research and is given a particular rationalisation, an explanation for how it has come about. This change does not 'just happen'; it is made to happen via a machine that reads brain-wave patterns and reproduces them in another brain. This is not to say, quite, that Watson's metamorphosis is 'scientific', where Kafka's is, we might say, 'arbitrary' or 'magical'. Science today could not effect the sort of change upon which Watson's book is premised, and it is a moot question whether it ever will be able to. It is equally impossible, in strict scientific terms, to manipulate DNA to create dinosaurs in the ways required by Michael Crichton's book *Jurassic Park* (1993), or to design spaceships that can travel between the stars like *Star Trek*'s USS Enterprise. But it is part of the logic of SF, and not of other forms of fiction, that these changes be made plausible within the structure of the text. This means that the premise of an SF novel requires material, physical rationalisation, rather than a supernatural or arbitrary one. This grounding of SF in the material rather than the supernatural becomes one of its key features. Sometimes this materialism is rooted in a 'scientific' outlook – science is, after all, one of the dominant materialist discourses of the present day. But sometimes the materialism is not, strictly speaking, scientific. Stephen Baxter's *Titan* (1998) is a novel about a journey of space exploration to Jupiter. Everything that happens in that novel adheres strictly to scientific laws as Baxter understands them – his characters even reuse the tried-and-tested technology of the Saturn V Moon programme from the 1970s. Kim Stanley Robinson's *Red Mars* (1992) also begins with a journey of exploration to another planet, again carefully imagined so as not to violate the constraints of current science and technology. Later in

Robinson's novel a technique is discovered for hugely extending human life span. This is certainly not within the discourse of current science, and may well be impossible, but the plot development is integrated into the pseudo-scientific idiom of the book. Instead of just asserting without explaining, as a magic-realist or surrealist writer might, that his characters can now postpone growing old for hundreds of years, Robinson introduces a material device, a gene resplicing bath, to explain and make plausible this idea.

To give another example of the contrast between SF and other fiction: John Updike's magic-realist novel *Brazil* (1994) tells the story of two lovers, a black boy and a white girl. In the course of the novel, the skin colours of these two figures change such that by the end of the book the boy is white and the girl black. This change is not rationalised in terms of the fictional world the characters inhabit, which is in all other respects a closely observed representation of contemporary South America; it is exactly the kind of unexplained literary device we associate with magic realism. On the other hand, there is a novel by John Kessel called *Good News from Outer Space* (1989) set in the near-future USA, one part of which is concerned with a new drug which alters skin pigmentation. Characters in the novel plan to release this drug in the American water supply as a terrorist gesture to undermine the ingrained racism of their society. Once again, we are tempted to call Kessel's book science fiction and Updike's not. Although both books are making points about the arbitrariness of racial definition by positing an interchangeability of skin colour, Kessel provides a specific mechanism for this change and Updike does not. Kessel's imaginary drug is not scientific – it does not and probably could not actually exist – but it is a material device and within the realm of the discourse it inhabits it is a plausible facilitator. Kessel's science fiction depends upon a certain premise, and that premise is symbolic of change. In other words, the drug is a symbol in terms of the text, but it is a concrete and material symbol that is integrated into a certain discourse of scientific possibility. Updike's text dispenses with the need for such a symbol.

It seems that this 'point of difference', the thing or things that differentiate the world portrayed in science fiction from the world we recognise around us, is the crucial separator between SF and other forms of imaginative or fantastic literature. The critic Darko Suvin has usefully coined the term 'novum', the Latin for 'new' or 'new thing', to refer to this 'point of difference' (the plural is 'nova'). An SF text may be based on one novum, such as the device that enables H.G. Wells's hero to travel through time in *The Time Machine* (1895). More usually it will be predicated on a number of interrelated nova, such as the varieties of futuristic technology found aboard the starship Enterprise in *Star Trek*, from faster-than-light travel to matter-transportation machines. This 'novum' must not be supernatural but need not necessarily be a piece of technology. The central 'novum' of Ursula Le Guin's *The Left Hand of Darkness* (1969), for instance, is a different model of gender, although there are other, more technological, 'nova' in that book, including inter-stellar transport and a hyperspace walkie-talkie called an 'ansible'. Unlike such premises as the human inexplicably metamorphosed into an insect in Kafka's story, these nova are grounded in a discourse of pos-sibility, which is usually science or technology and which renders the difference a material rather than just a conceptual or imaginative one. The emphasis is on difference, and the systematic working out of the consequences of a difference or differences, of a novum or nova, becomes the strength of the mode.

THREE DEFINITIONS

There have been a great many attempts to define science fiction in more exact terms than these. Once we accept that the particularities of the 'novum' distinguish SF from other forms of imaginative literature, the urge is to expand upon the sorts of literary context in which these nova are elaborated – to flesh out, in other words, the broader features of the SF text beyond its notional, material point of difference with our famil-iar world.

It is worth detailing three definitions of SF that have been particu-larly influential on the study of the subject, from three influential crit-ics: Darko Suvin, Robert Scholes and Damien Broderick. First, there is respected elder statesman of SF criticism Darko Suvin, who in 1979 defined SF as:

> a literary genre or verbal construct whose necessary and sufficient condi-tions are the *presence and interaction of estrangement and cognition,*

and whose main device is an imaginative framework alternative to the author's empirical environment.

(Suvin 1988: 37)

'Cognition', with its rational, logical implications, refers to that aspect of SF that prompts us to try and understand, to comprehend, the alien landscape of a given SF book, film or story. 'Estrangement' is a term from Brecht, more usually rendered in English-language criticism as 'alienation'; in this context it refers to that element of SF that we recognise as different, that 'estranges' us from the familiar and everyday. If the SF text were entirely concerned with 'estrangement', then we would not be able to understand it; if it were entirely to do with 'cognition', then it would be scientific or documentary rather than science fiction. According to Suvin, both features need to be present; and it is this co-presence that allows SF both relevance to our world and the position to challenge the ordinary, the taken-for-granted. The main 'formal device' of Suvin's version of SF is the novum.

Suvin goes on to insist that this 'alternative' world of SF, determined by 'estrangement' *and* 'cognition', must be possible, by which he means it must reflect the constraints of science. This is how he distinguishes SF from the looser category of 'fantasy'; and indeed, he often seems to have little respect for 'fantasy' precisely because it lacks 'cognitive plausibility'. It might perhaps be argued that 'cognitive' is almost a synonym for 'scientific', that his phrase 'cognitive estrangement' is just another way of restating the phrase that is to be defined, 'science fiction'. One of the strengths of Suvin's definition is that it seems to embody a certain common-sense tautology, that science fiction is scientific fictionalising. But, as we have seen, science is just as frequently represented in the SF novel by pseudo-science, by some device outside the boundaries of science that is none the less rationalised in the *style* of scientific discourse. We might want to define 'science' as a body of observations and derived laws established by experiment in the real world; but, according to this definition, several of the frequently deployed 'nova' of SF are things that 'science' has specifically ruled out of court as literally impossible. The most obvious example of this is faster-than-light travel, a staple of a great many SF tales but something that scientists assure us can never happen. Rather than abandon the rationale of science, though, SF stories that involve 'faster-than-light' travel slip into the idiom of 'pseudo-science', providing rationalisations of these impossible activities in terms that *sound* like scientific discourse.

For Suvin, the important thing about the 'science' part of 'science fiction' is that it is a discourse built on certain logical principles that avoids self-contradiction; that it is rational rather than emotional or instinctual. Scientists sometimes like to assert that they deal in 'facts' and 'truth', where fiction deals in 'imagination' and is a form of lying. But it is more accurate to describe science as a discipline based on falsifiability, a discourse in which hypotheses are tested by experiment. Accordingly, whilst a scientific premise may be proved false, it cannot be proved true. In science fiction it is not that the use of science gives the texts a particular, privileged access to truth. Often the reverse is true. Gwyneth Jones points out that Larry Niven's *Ringworld* (1970), 'one of the great, classic "engineering feat" SF novels, reached print in the first instance with terrible mistakes in its science' (Jones 1999: 16). Niven revised the novel for subsequent publication after fans pointed out a number of scientific impossibilities, but Jones makes the point that 'the challenge, which had to be met, was not to Niven's scientific accuracy, but to his appearance of command over the *language* of science'. Many early SF novels followed the scientific thinking of the day and imagined canals on Mars, oceans on Venus. The fact that more recent scientific experiment has concluded that there are no such canals or oceans does not invalidate these novels, because the point about the science in SF is not 'truth' but the entry into a particular, material and often rational discourse. We might indeed see SF as a form of thought experiment, an elaborate 'what if?' game, where the consequences of some or other novum are worked through. In other words, it is not the 'truth' of science that is important to SF; it is the scientific method, the logical working through of a particular premise. This is precisely what Suvin asserts: 'SF is distinguished by the narrative dominance or hegemony of a fictional 'novum' ... validated by cognitive logic' (Suvin 1979: 63). By this he means that the implications of the 'novum' dominate, or create a 'hegemony' (a term from Marxist theory to describe the maintenance of power by indirect and pervasive means rather than by direct force) throughout the text. 'Cognitive Logic' becomes for Suvin a crucial formal convention of SF.

If Suvin takes his starting point from the 'science' part of 'science fiction', another highly influential critic has concentrated more on the literary features of SF texts. Robert Scholes, in his book *Structural Fabulation*, has stressed the metaphorical strain of SF. He defines 'fabulation' as any 'fiction that offers us a world clearly and radically discontinuous from the one we know, yet returns to confront that known world in some cognitive way' (Scholes 1975: 2). This point of 'discontinuity' with the known world is the Suvinian novum, but Scholes inflects this rather differently. He wants to acknowledge that SF is interested in things being different from the world we actually inhabit, but does not want to concede that this makes SF merely escapist or irrelevant. According to Scholes, SF is both different and the same, both 'discontinuous' from our world and also 'confronting' that world 'in some cognitive way'. Scholes notes that 'fabulation' is a category including any and all fantastic or imaginative literature, including non-SF writers like Borges, Thomas Pynchon and Herman Hesse, to mention three of Scholes's own examples. Accordingly, Scholes adds 'structural' to his 'fabulation' definition in order to pin things down more tightly. As with Suvin, there's a certain re-duplication here. 'Fabulation' seems synonymous with 'fiction' in pretty much the same way that 'structural' is with science; we could abbreviate both 'science fiction' and 'structural fabulation' to SF if we wanted to. In fact, Scholes's point is a little more subtle than that. For him, SF is permeated by 'an awareness of the universe as a system of systems, a structure of structures'. Whilst he concedes that, for SF, 'the insights of the past century of science are accepted as fictional points of departure', he is none the less adamant that SF is more than just a 'scientific' version of fabulation. 'Structural fabulation is neither scientific in its methods, nor a substitute for actual science. It is a fictional exploration of human situations made perceptible by the implications of recent science.' (Scholes 1975: 8). One of the reasons Scholes thinks so highly of SF is because of the possibilities it opens up as a distinctive, twentieth-century 'scientific' mode of literature. More particularly, 'science', which is an observational method, is only the starting point for Scholes's SF. He is more interested in the fictionalisation of the premise, and accordingly his emphasis is rather different from Suvin's.

This 'scientific' – cognitive, rational, categorical – approach to the issues of defining the genre has the upper hand in much critical discus-

sion of SF. Damien Broderick, an SF author as well as being a theoreti-
cally engaged critic, concludes his analysis of the contemporary SF scene
with the following definition of what SF is now:

> Sf is that species of storytelling native to a culture undergoing the epis-
> temic changes implicated in the rise and supercession of technical–
> industrial modes of production, distribution, consumption and dis-
> posal. It is marked by (i) metaphoric strategies and metonymic tac-
> tics, (ii) the foregrounding of icons and interpretative schemata from
> a collectively constituted generic 'mega-text' and the concomitant de-
> emphasis of 'fine writing' and characterisation, and (iii) certain priori-
> ties more often found in scientific and postmodern texts than in
> literary models: specifically, attention to the object in preference to
> the subject.
>
> (Broderick 1995: 155)

The sheer complexity of this definition enacts the pseudo-scientific
discourse that is also at the heart of much SF. Indeed, it is so complex
that it would take many pages for me to unpack all the terminology of
this definition, although I discuss one key element of it, 'metaphoric
strategies and metonymic tactics', at length in Chapter 6. But one
point is worth dwelling on for a moment; Broderick's insight that we
recognise SF in part because it deploys certain 'icons' that are consensually taken as 'SF'. Many of these devices, as Broderick mentions,
derive from a corpus of accepted 'nova': starships, time-machines,
robots and the like. Each of these connects with a particular 'estranged'
version of our reality.

Broderick develops and deepens the Suvinian sense of 'cognitive
estrangement' and Scholes's 'structural fabulation'; but he also brings in
aspects not dwelt upon by either of those critics. In particular, he is very
aware of SF as a *popular* genre, one that shares many features with other
'pulp' fictions and popular modes, what he calls a 'de-emphasis on fine
writing' and the use of a range of accepted or even worn-out conventional 'icons': the mad scientist, say, or the robot yearning for humanity.
Lurking behind this is a sense that SF is popular because it is populist,
that it panders to the lowest common denominator, that it is an adolescent mode of writing, that it is not 'serious' or 'high art'.

Broderick's perspective here is part of a larger critical unease about SF as a genre, a sense that it does not provide readers with many of the things that serious literature does: for instance, beautiful or experimental writing styles, detailed and subtle analyses of character or psychological analyses. It may be possible to think of SF texts that do these things, but most do not. Instead of style, SF texts often concentrate on concept, subject and narrative. Instead of the abstract, SF texts prefer the concrete, so, rather than meditate upon 'alienness', a SF novel is more likely to present us with an actual, concretely realised alien, with blue skin and bug eyes. According to SF author and critic Gwyneth Jones, SF avoids the trappings of mainstream fiction so as not to distract its readership from the conceptual experiment it represents; fine writing is 'de-emphasised' in order to allow content and concept to come more obviously to the fore. 'A typical science fiction novel has little space for deep and studied characterisation,' argues Jones, 'not because writers lack the skill (although they may) but because in the final analysis the characters are not people, they are pieces of equipment ... the same reductive effect is at work on the plot, where naked, artless ur-scenarios of quest, death and desire are openly displayed' (Jones 1999: 5). This is a version of Broderick's suggestion that SF is more interested in 'object' than subject.

It is hard to deny that many SF texts are limited and narrow if judged by the aesthetic criteria sometimes applied to other literatures; that their characterisation often is thin, their style dull and unadventurous, their plots hackneyed. Moreover, the nova that differentiate the SF world from the recognisable world of realist fiction are more often than not drawn from a fairly narrow range of stock themes and situations. In fact, it is possible to classify the major tropes of SF into half a dozen categories. Books that take any of the following subjects, themes, trappings or props are liable to be thought of as science fiction:

- spaceships, interplanetary or interstellar travel
- aliens and the encounter with aliens
- mechanical robots, genetic engineering, biological robots
- computers, advanced technology, virtual reality
- time travel
- alternative history
- futuristic utopias and dystopias.

A body of literature built on so narrow a base of premises runs the risk of becoming, in practice, repetitive and crude, and Broderick sometimes gives the impression that he is picking only a few exceptional texts from a morass of formulaic and mass-market examples. He talks of 'the poverty of mass-market SF' being 'visible even in the new work of attested and once-fresh writers' of the calibre of Asimov.

There can certainly be a wearying sense of déjà vu in reading a new SF novel. Broderick himself quotes the blurbs from recent SF publishers' catalogues to illustrate that SF nova have in large part lost all newness because of their endless circulation and recirculation:

CYBERSTEALTH, S. N. Lewitt – The cyberstealth pilots are the best of the breed. But Cargo, the best of the best, needs more than expert flying to seek and destroy a traitor.

REVENGE OF THE VALKYRIE, Thorarinn Gunnarsson – Here is the blazing epic sequel to Song of the Dwarves.

GUARDIANS OF THE THREE VOL II. KEEPER OF THE CITY, Bill Fawcett – This is a magnificent epic of adventure, romance and wizardry set in the unique world of the catlike mrem.

BROTHER TO DEMONS, BROTHER TO GODS, Jack Williamson – From the test tubes of a dying humanity comes the first of a race of gods.

(Broderick 1995: 11–12)

Broderick considers these 'hilariously awful ... blazing sequel to dwarves, indeed!', but there is a serious point, too. As he observes, it is 'one of the comforts of this list, for habituated readers', that 'the catlike mrem live in a world which is precisely not unique' (Broderick 1995: 12). Many fans of SF seek out the comfort of the familiar and mask that desire under the illusory rhetoric of difference, of 'catlike mrem' and their like.

This helps us draw these different definitions towards some sort of common conclusion. It seems that one of the axes of critical enquiry has to do with the degree of proximity of the 'difference' of SF to the world we live in: too removed and the SF text loses purchase, becomes impossible for the reader to identify with or care about the imaginary world portrayed; too close and it might as well be a conventional novel, it loses the force and penetration the novum can possess when it comes to providing newness of perspective. Balancing 'cognition' and 'estrangement', or the continuities and discontinuities of the SF text, becomes the index of success of the SF text. More than this, it seems that this balance is focused through the novum. In other words, implicit within these three definitions is a sense of SF as a *symbolist* genre, one where the novum acts as symbolic manifestation of something that connects it specifically with the world we live in, the attempt to represent the world within reproducing it in its own terms. Suvin puts the emphasis here, describing SF as 'a symbolic system' which is 'centred on a novum which is to be cognitively validated within the narrative reality of the tale' (Suvin 1979: 80).

There are important differences in seeing SF as symbolist rather than allegorical. Symbolism opens itself up to a richness of possible interpretation, where allegory maps significance from one thing on to one other thing. More than this, any symbolist movement in literature, such as the late nineteenth-century movement of symbolist poetry, will tend to reuse a fairly limited corpus of symbols. M. H. Abrams lists some of the recurring icons of nineteenth-century symbolist writing, 'such as the morning and evening star, a boat moving upstream, winding caves, and the conflict between a serpent and an eagle' (Abrams 1985: 186). He goes on to quote symbolist poet Baudelaire to the effect that symbolism draws on 'the correspondences' between 'the spiritual and the natural world'. The point of SF, on the other hand, is to be less spiritual and more material, and accordingly this line of criticism enables us to look again at the limited range of nova deployed in most science fiction not as a narrow and exhausted set of clichés, but as a supple and wide-referencing body of material symbols. The catlike mrem, for example, can be seen less as a feeble rehashing of worn-out tropes and more as a fictional inhabiting – successful or not depending on the skill with which the author deploys these emblems – of a potent SF symbol of alienness.

The obvious point of contrast might be thought to be with a deliberately non-symbolist mode of writing, such as 'realism'. Realist fiction seeks to reproduce the experience of living in a particular milieu exactly, and often exhaustively, and aims for a sense of documentary verisimilitude. But in a strange way, SF has more in common with realism than it has with other, more obviously imaginative, mainstream literatures. To elaborate this point it is worth noting that 'realism' is only one form of mainstream writing; much ordinary fiction introduces 'symbolic' devices, various imaginative strategies to provide 'discontinuities' with our experience of the world, without thereby becoming science fiction. But the textual function of these nova in SF sets them apart from other usage. In other words, SF gives us a unique version of the symbolist approach, one where the symbol is drained of transcendental or metaphysical aura and relocated back in the material world. For example, a 'realist' novel like Emile Zola's *Germinal* (1885) creates a sense of what it was actually like to live in a nineteenth-century French mining community by accumulating a great deal of accurately observed material detail. By contrast, a non-realist modernist novel like Virginia Woolf's *The Waves* (1931) is built around the stream-of-consciousness meanderings of its six characters. Instead of a large amount of realistic material detail, Woolf concentrates on certain recurring symbolic images, such as the sun rising and setting over a seascape, or the fin of a fish breaking the surface of the waves. Science fiction is symbolic, but it usually adopts the realist mode of an accumulation of detail, rather than the poetic and lyrical method of a writer like Woolf. To quote Suvin again, the symbolic novum 'has to be convincingly explained in concrete, even if imaginary, terms, that is, in terms of the specific time, place, agents, and cosmic and social totality of each tale'. Suvin goes on to note that 'this means that, in principle, SF has to be judged, like most naturalistic or "realistic" fiction and quite unlike [supernatural] horror fantasy, by the density and richness of objects and agents described in the microcosm of the text' (Suvin 1979: 80). The attention to detail and the density of the described reality in many SF texts mean that, very often, they read like realist novels; or perhaps a better phrase would be pseudo-realist. But the crucial point is that science fiction reconfigures symbolism for our materialist age.

It is this materialism, once again, that distinguishes the effectiveness of the SF use of symbol from the widespread use of symbolism in other literatures. To take another example, the trope of the 'invisible man' is one we might think of as a classic SF novum. H G Wells wrote a short novel on this theme in 1897. The difference between this SF text and Ralph Ellison's celebrated novel of Black American experience, also called *Invisible Man* (1952) – a book never described as SF – has to do with the operation of this novum in the text itself. Ellison's protagonist is invisible because people simply don't see him, and they don't see him because he is black. Ellison's point, in other words, is to express metaphorically, through the trope of the invisible man, the social invisibility and alienation that are part of the experience of being black in America. Wells's protagonist, on the other hand, is a scientist. His invisibility is specifically rationalised as the result of scientific research. The particular alienation experienced by Wells's invisible man stems from his own antisocial personality, which in turn is an expression of the way science denies common nature and humanity. Ellison's invisibility is a transcendent device, in the sense of being something that transcends or passes beyond conventional literary expectations; it is a means of metaphorically apprehending the experience of a whole group of people. Wells's is a concrete symbol of the dehumanisation of science, a particular coding of the very materiality of science's practice. Both have things to say about the real world, but the two works go about this in different manners.

DIFFERENCE

The problematic of this encounter with difference, the difficulty of representing the other without losing touch with the familiar, becomes exactly the point of some of the most celebrated SF texts. It is possible to explore the strangeness and threat of the other without surrendering to two-dimensional caricature of otherness as evil. A classic example is Stanislaw Lem's novel *Solaris* (1961), set aboard a research station on another planet, a planet almost entirely covered with a strange ocean. It seems that this ocean is sentient, making the whole world a sort of giant brain. The scientist-protagonists of Lem's tale are trying to comprehend this unprecedented place, trying, in other words, to reduce it to the sameness of scientific explanation. But the world defies comprehension; it sends out hallucinations of people important to the scientists. The contact drives some of them mad. Snow, one of the occupants of the station, comes to an important realisation late in the novel and anatomises the human urge to explore the universe:

> We don't want to conquer the cosmos, we simply want to extend the boundaries of Earth to the frontiers of the cosmos. For us, such and such a planet is as arid as the Sahara, another as frozen as the North Pole, yet another as lush as the Amazon basin ... We are only seeking Man. We have no need of other worlds. We need mirrors.
>
> (Lem, *Solaris* (1961): 75–6)

The ocean-planet of Solaris, in its strangeness and unpredictability, denies this devouring urge to transmute all alterity into versions of sameness, and that is why the scientists cannot cope with it. The perfectly judged tone of uncanny uncertainty in Lem's novel, the way it consistently refuses the straightforward explanation of the characters' situation, precisely captures the way encountering the other forces us to encounter ourselves, the way it can reveal things about ourselves which are intensely uncomfortable. 'We arrive here as we are in reality, and when the page is turned and that reality is revealed to us – that part of our reality which we would prefer to pass over in silence – then we don't like it any more' (p. 76).

What these various definitions of SF have in common, then, is a sense of SF as in some central way about the encounter with difference. This encounter is articulated through a 'novum', a conceptual, or more usually material, embodiment of alterity, the point at which the SF text distils the difference between its imagined world and the world which we all inhabit. For Scott McCracken, 'at the root of all science fiction lies the fantasy of alien encounter'. He adds that 'the meeting of self with other is perhaps the most fearful, most exciting and most erotic encounter of all' (McCracken 1998: 102). This serves as the basis of many critics' affection for the genre, the fact that SF provides a means, in a popular and accessible fictional form, for exploring alterity. Specific SF nova are more than just gimmicks, and much more than clichés; they provide a symbolic grammar for articulating the perspectives of normally marginalised discourses of race, of gender, of non-conformism and alternative ideologies. We might think of this as the progressive or radical potential of science fiction.

But it is not necessarily clear that SF is as positive a mode as this optimistic assessment suggests. Even if we set aside the more obviously retrograde examples of SF that introduce difference only to demonise it, some critics are not sanguine about the ability of the genre to access otherness. Damien Broderick, for instance, wonders if SF does, 'above all else, write the narrative of the other/s?', but goes on to say that even if we take that 'in the spirit of description (though hardly of definition)', we still have to accept that 'SF writes, rather, the narrative of the same, as other' (Broderick 1995: 51). Could we argue that all these SF nova, from aliens to machines, are merely elaborations of a monolithic conception of Identity?

The demographics of the genre are not hopeful in this regard. Until relatively recently, SF was dominated by a fan culture of young white males. Science fiction's tendency to make a fetish of technology, particularly military technology, and its reliance on stock types of character and plot that are often flat and two dimensional surely limit its engagement with any meaningful comprehension of the marginal, of otherness. But there are features of this readership that start to redeem it: the energy of youth, for example, has a part to play in constructing SF as, to quote Roger Luckhurst, 'an adolescent and exuberantly kinetic genre' (Luckhurst 1997: 4). Indeed, despite the strong attachment of SF to its own canonical conventions and the tendency of much SF tacitly to accept dominant ideological and political belief systems, the genre has always had sympathies with the marginal and the different. Gary Westfahl admits that 'science fiction [is] regularly condemned as the quintessentially masculine genre, long written almost exclusively by and for young men, filled with muscle-bound macho heroes swaggering and bullying their way through the galaxy'. But, Westfahl argues, the reality is not at all like this, because in fact SF has what he calls a 'feminine' aura. He itemises the way that American SF from the 1940s and 1950s – the so-called 'Golden Age' of SF – demonstrated remarkable sensitivities on the subjects of gender and racial diversity and contact, and asks:

> Why should this be, given the undeniable fact that most of the writers and readers were male? Well, the young nerds attracted to science fiction may have shared the gender and skin-colour of the era's dominant class, but in every other way they were alienated and marginalized members of society, dreaming of domed cities and Martian canals when most people longed for an idealized past and

idolized [cowboy icons] Gene Autry and Andy Hardy. If, at that time, you read magazines with pictures of squid-like monsters and built miniature rockets in your backyard, you undoubtedly felt rejected, ridiculed, and out of place. Such people often bond with, and adopt the attitudes of, other members of society who feel rejected, ridiculed, and out of place. By this logic, one would expect to find in early science-fiction stories passionate arguments against prejudice and racism, celebrations of oppressed workers struggling against evil bosses, and proto-feminist tracts applauding the abilities and sentiments of women. And if you look carefully, you will find, in the science fiction of the 1930s and thereafter, numerous examples of all the above.

(Westfahl 1999: 32)

Reading SF, in other words, is about reading the marginal experience coded through the discourses of material symbolism; which is to say, it allows the symbolic expression of what it is to be female, or black, or otherwise marginalised. SF, by focusing its representations of the world not through *reproduction* of that world but instead by figuratively symbolising it, is able to foreground precisely the ideological constructions of otherness. In other words, in societies such as ours where otherness is often demonised, SF can pierce the constraints of this ideology by circumventing the conventions of traditional fiction.

A film such as *Lost in Space* (1998) represents a number of 'nova' and a variety of versions of difference; but at the same time it is so scared of difference that all possible manifestations of it need to be fully demonised and then utterly vanquished. Sameness in this movie is tightly defined as 'belonging to the white family unit'; every good quantity encountered in the film either belongs to the family or is adopted by it – from the cute baby-like alien adopted by the family to the space pilot who is courting the blonde, blue-eyed, scientist's daughter. Everything that is not 'of the family' is represented as evil and threatening. The hidden agenda here, it seems to me, is racial. The Robinson family are so egregiously White that all representations of blackness become freighted with particular significance. When the fey English villain is bitten by a being from a breed of half-organic, half-machine, alien monsters, he is metamorphosed into something terrible:

'evil always finds its true form', as Papa Robinson puts it. Its true form in this instance is that of a towering black man, who paces menacingly around the margins of the family, having perpetrated some unspeakable doom upon Will Robinson's mother and sister ('I can still hear the screaming of the women,' says a traumatised Will). The Robinsons are certainly encountering difference, but only in the limited sense of racial caricature, a violent, sexually predatory libel on black manhood. Difference, in other words, has been reduced to stereotype, and stereotype is always at the bottom of racism, sexism or any other bigotry. Ultimately, this black threat to the White family is flushed down a cosmic plughole like the rubbish he is represented as being, and the family is reunited to its stifling conformity. Here the symbolic field of signification seems racial, something that we examine in more detail in Chapter 4. This is one example of many in SF of a refusal to think through the implications of encountering difference. Not all SF is so crude or bigoted.

STRUCTURALIST APPROACHES

The logic behind these sorts of definition is basically *structuralist*. Structuralism is the name given to a loose affiliation of critics and scholars whose approach to the business of criticism dominated academies in the 1960s and early 1970s. Linguists had shown that the many different specific languages spoken in the world can be analysed in terms of a complex but consistent set of grammatical and syntactical rules underpinning them all. Structuralist critics such as Roland Barthes or Gérard Genette attempted to apply this approach to literature and culture as well as language, claiming to uncover, for instance, the underlying grammar of narrative (we are probably all familiar with the idea that all stories can be seen as variations on seven fundamental patterns), or of cultural forms more generally. Structuralist literary criticism was, in part, a reaction to older forms of criticism premised on ideas of 'the genius the author', stressing instead literature as a system of signification.

At the risk of oversimplifying a complicated period in academic history, structuralism was superseded in most universities during the 1980s by 'post-structuralism' or 'deconstruction', a set of more radical and philosophically nuanced critical strategies that denied the universal-ising, pseudo-scientific claims of structuralism. Insightful if obscure critics such as Jacques Derrida and Paul de Man insisted instead on close readings of the particularity of literature, an attention to the margins of texts and an understanding of the radical instability of the very categories structuralist critics had tried to establish as universals.

It is probably true to say most critics of SF, even those working currently, are more influenced by structuralist assumptions than post-structuralist ones. The magisterial and indispensable *Encyclopedia of Science Fiction* (second edition 1993, edited by John Clute and Peter Nicholls), whilst acknowledging the immense hybridity of SF with genres such as Fantasy, Horror, Techno-thriller and Magic Realism, nevertheless attempts to establish the categories 'fundamental to SF'. Much of the critical discussion about SF, for instance online, worries away obsessively about what is and what isn't 'proper' science fiction, establishing sets of conceptual pigeonholes as an implicit grammar of the genre. Many critical studies of SF are, in essence, taxonomies. Indeed, given the hospitality to otherness that ought to be a feature of the best SF, it is rather dispiriting to see so many SF critics labouring so strenuously to establish a 'pure race' model of what SF is. Moreover, it is probably true to say that 'deconstruction' is taken by many readers today, and some critics as well, as a byword for wilful obscurity and meaningless jargonised flapdoodle.

But it is worth rehearsing, in brief, why so many academic critics fell under the spell of deconstruction in the 1980s, and the ways in which structuralist critical conventions came to be seen as flawed. The impulse towards systematic categorisation of any literature, whilst superficially beguiling, is dangerously flattening and distorting in practice. For example, a recent neo-structuralist study by Christopher Brooker claimed to codify, as its title declares, *The Seven Basic Plots* (2004). The first of Brooker's archetypal stories, 'Overcoming the Monster', is presented as a timeless category, including both the old-English poem *Beowulf* and the late twentieth-century SF film *The Terminator* (1984) as examples. Brooker's self-satisfaction, evident throughout his book, can be shared by the reader who notices, perhaps for the first time, that – yes, those two texts are based on very similar premises: young hero must fight seemingly indestructible monster, eventually defeating him. There are, as Brooker points out, thousands of similar stories. But the satisfaction of sorting all those stories into that one conceptual drawer is a puerile one, the delight of the child who notices for the first time that human beings, monkeys and shopfront dummies are all similar. Because the inescapable fact is that, having read *Beowulf*, we do not load *Terminator* into the DVD player for 'more of the same'. We go to specific texts for their specificities. Although there are similarities between *Beowulf* and the *Terminator*, there are very many more points of difference, and it is those differences, the particularised intensities and localised qualia of actual textual production, that provide us without our major satisfactions. Here are three SF texts: Kurt Vonnegut's novel *Slaughterhouse-Five* (1969), the TV series *Quantum Leap* (1989–1993) and the recent bestseller by Audrey Niffenegger, *The Time Traveler's Wife* (2004). All three of these share the same novum: a character who has come loose in time, in some sense, and whose consciousness is hurtled backwards and forwards within the time frame of their own life, or only a little way beyond it. But although the structuralist temptation is to file all three away in the same pigeonhole, in fact these are three radically different texts. The Vonnegut is a profound and thought-provoking meditation on the experience of the Second World War, and civilian mass murder in particular, that achieves its uniquely moving effect through a brilliantly handled deadpan deftness of style. The TV series is a witty, bizarre and entertaining conceit that enables a disconnected series of dramatic set pieces. The Niffenegger novel is a conventional contemporary-set love story that uses its SF novum as garnish to an otherwise rather ordinary tale of the tribulations of courtship. Any criticism that blurs the very different particularities of these texts is, at the least, lacking in nuance and, at the worst, a positively unhelpful way of looking at culture.

To instance one more attempt at defining SF. Gary Westfahl is a better informed and more intelligent critic than many, yet even he can come up with a definition as procrustean as this:

> Science fiction is a twentieth-century literary genre consisting of texts labelled 'science fiction' which are associated with explicit or implicit claims that each of its labelled texts has these three narrative traits:

A. It is a prose narrative.
B. It includes language which either describes scientific facts, or explains or reflects the processes of scientific thought; and
C. It describes or depicts some aspect or development which does not exist at the time of writing.

(Westfahl 1998)

This is a definition that serves Westfahl's purposes and includes all the SF that he is interested in discussing. But what about the SF it explicitly excludes? What, for instance, about the film *Star Wars* (1977), the play *R.U.R, Rossum's Universal Robots* (1920), the graphic novel *Watchmen* (1987), the work of musician Sun-Ra, such as *We Travel the Spaceways* (1965), the video game *Doom* (1993), the SF concept album *Time* (1981) by ELO, or the paintings of British artist Chris Foss? Not to mention novels such as David Lindsay's *A Voyage to Arcturus* (1920), which offends Westfahl's rubric under 'B', or novels like Philip Dick's *The Man in the High Castle* (1962) and William Gibson and Bruce Sterling's *The Difference Engine* (1990), which offend Westfahl's rubric under 'C'?

The temptation, once a critic has established a definition, is for him or her simply to dismiss texts which fall outside it as 'not truly SF', a circular logic that can become self-sustaining. The case is similar to a joke from Douglas Adams' very popular SF radio serial *The Hitch-Hiker's Guide to the Galaxy* (1978–80) – another text not SF by Westfahl's definition – in which the fabulous prosperity of a certain planet is described as so comprehensive that 'nobody was really poor; at least, nobody worth mentioning'. This runs the risk of opening up a sort of critical binary: 'SF classics' that the critics include as respectable, and material that is ignored as not really SF, or not worthy of critical attention. But SF, whatever it is, is not a binary; it is a multiplicity of complexly interacting discourses, each of which contains material good, bad and indifferent.

At the beginning of the chapter I quoted, amongst the many bickering versions of 'a definition of SF', Damon Knight's tautological statement: 'science fiction is what we point to when we say it'. Strangely enough, this approach at defining the genre might be more useful than Westfahl's more deeply thought-through schema. The problem with it is that, of itself, it gives us no purchase on two key terms: who 'we' are and what the 'it' is at which we are pointing, when we point at 'it'. But, a little tentatively, we can start by saying that 'we' are the people who are interested in SF: fans, readers, critics, students. And we can add that amongst the things we point at are texts like *Star Wars* and graphic novels like *Watchmen* as well as many novels and short stories. One of the most important features of this 'we' is precisely that it includes difference, that it is not defined by monolithic agreement. When Neal Stephenson's novel *Quicksilver* (2003) won the prestigious Arthur C Clarke award in 2004, many greeted it as a masterpiece, but some contended that, set as it is wholly within a detailed historical reconstruction of the late seventeenth century, it is not really science fiction. The Clarke judges clearly thought it was and recognised its excellence. In the words of Farah Mendlesohn, 'science fiction is less a genre … than an ongoing discussion' (James and Mendlesohn 2003: 1).

PREDICTION AND NOSTALGIA

These difficulties of defining SF are, in part, a function of the sheer number of SF texts that need to be brought beneath the bar of any notional inclusive definition. Where SF once upon a time constituted a small body of texts, nearly all of them novels and short stories, which most fans could be expected to have read, nowadays SF texts are impossibly legion. Scott McCracken points out that 'Science Fiction is enormously popular. It accounts for one in ten books sold in Britain, and in the United States the number is as high as one in four' (McCracken 1998: 102). John Clute has pointed out that the number of texts classified as SF has ballooned since the early years of the twentieth century. According to Clute, even at the height of the 'Golden Age' the number of separate novels published as science fiction was a few hundred a year. Nowadays, taking together science fiction and fantasy, thousands of novels are published annually. Now 'what was once a field [has] become the Mississippi Delta'. In Clute's opinion, if Golden Age SF could be perceived as '*a family of books* which created (and inhabited) a knowable stage (or matrix) of possible worlds', then contemporary SF has exploded that family: 'no longer could an ostensible definition of SF … even begin to match the corrosive intricacies of the exploded genre' (Clute 1995: 17–18).

SF, then, clearly constitutes a wide range of varying discourses, so wide a range indeed that it becomes difficult to assert that all the different manifestations of 'SF' actually belong under the one umbrella term, not merely in terms of genre or mode, short stories, novels, films, TV shows, comics, video games, pop music and so on, but in the broader sense of cultural discourse. Talking about NASA's space programme, or the present construction of the International Space Station, automatically, it seems, inhabits the idiom of SF; and the number of New Age or mystical belief systems that have replaced conventional religion with a belief in one or another SF prop is remarkable, from abduction-enthusiasts who believe the Earth to be in the care of spiritually intense aliens, to cults that practise mass suicide in the belief that their souls will be carried away by an alien spacecraft hidden in a comet.

This was not always the case. In the so-called 'Golden Age' of science fiction, from the late 1930s through to the early 1960s, the term 'science fiction' had a greater degree of coherence. It referred to a particular body of texts that were, specifically, founded in science and the extrapolation of science into the future. Hugo Gernsback (1884–1967), founder of a number of influential SF magazines, inserted an editorial into the first number of his *Science Wonder Stories* (June 1929) in which he declared his 'policy' to be the publishing of 'only such stories that have their basis in scientific laws as we know them, or in the logical deduction of new laws from what we know'. He went so far as to announce that a panel of experts would judge the scientific correctness of stories submitted to the magazine. But there has been a shift in the role of the scientific novum; it now connects its readership less with a particular discourse of 'science' and more, as I have been arguing, with a materialist, symbolic fiction for reconsidering the world. The balance, to reuse Scholes's distinction, has shifted towards the fabulation and away from the structural. As we have seen, the term 'science fiction' today suggests an imaginative fiction in which one or more of the contemporary constraints upon the business of living are removed or modified. John Clute sees 1957 as the significant historical moment, with the launch of the Russian satellite Sputnik.

> There may have been a time, in the morning of the world, before
> Sputnik, when the empires of our SF dreams were governed according

> to rules neatly written out in the pages of *Astounding*, and we could all play the game of a future we all shared, readers, writers, fans ... But something happened. The future began to come true.
>
> (Clute 1995: 17)

This has something to do with a certain shift in cultural sensibilities. Space flight changed from being a thing of a gleamingly imagined future to being real, and then went on to pass that by and become, as it is nowadays, a thing of *the past*. A film such as Ron Howard's *Apollo 13* (1996) illustrates this neatly enough. It is a film about the adventures of the crew of a spaceship, off on a perilous mission, who have to battle with near-fatal malfunction, and accordingly it is a film that follows a standard SF trajectory, one seen in such classic films as *2001: A Space Odyssey* (1968) and *Dark Star* (1974). But this is a text that looks *backwards* not forwards. The key thing, it seems to me, is less that the film is 'true' – although, of course, it is – but that the film is so specifically *historical*. The astonishing special effects that recreate what lift-off in Saturn V and a journey through space must have been like are paralleled in the film by a precise recreation of the early 1970s milieu that is the setting for the picture. Watching *Apollo 13* is an experience that parallels more straightforwardly science-fictional films in interesting ways; but watching it also creates an acute awareness that 'going to the Moon' was something our ancestors did, not something we do today or are going to do in the future.

What *Apollo 13* does, in fact, is epitomise an important argument about SF made by several critics: although many people think of SF as something that looks to the future, the truth is that most SF texts are more interested in the way things have been. SF uses the trappings of fantasy to explore again age-old issues; or, to put it another way, the chief mode of science fiction is not prophecy but nostalgia. That SF is not prophetic seems clear enough. There have been hundreds of thousands of SF texts throughout the twentieth century, but only very rarely – statistically no more than would be expected by the operations of chance – have any of those texts accurately predicted anything. Jules Verne predicted that men would fly to the Moon, blasting off from a location very close to Cape Canaveral in Florida; but he also thought that firing capsules out of cannons would be a good way of propelling people on this space voyage, when in fact the suddenness of the acceleration would squash the astronauts like bugs. H. G. Wells predicted the inventions of tanks and aerial bombing. But he didn't anticipate computers, didn't realise that life in space would be weightless, and confidently predicted that a world-wide government of scientists and rational men would create a global utopia by the 1950s. SF prediction is wrong far more than it is right, but we needn't be embarrassed on this account, because the recent developments in 'Chaos Theory' have taught us that the business of accurate prediction in a chaotic system like 'The World' is literally impossible. No, despite a surface attachment to 'the future', it seems clear that SF actually enacts a fascination with the past for which 'nostalgia' is the best description. *Star Wars* (1977) begins with the caption 'A Long Time Ago in a Galaxy Far Away ...', and the action of that film owes more to the past, and specifically to director George Lucas's youth, than to any coherently imagined future. His spaceships are more like warplanes, going off on sorties straight out of *633 Squadron* or *The Dam Busters*, than spaceships; this is why they make screaming and whooshing noises when flying though the noiseless vacuum of space. A spaceship would be silent, but the X-Wing fighters aren't really spaceships, they're Spitfires and P-51s. Frank Herbert's *Dune* (1965), one of the most famous SF novels of the postwar period, is also thoroughly grounded in this retro-vision. Despite being set in the 211th century, it introduces us to a world that owes more to a dream of Arabia in the Middle Ages than to any future we can plausibly conceive: a world without computers or science, a religious, mystical and superstitious world, a reactionary and intensely old-fashioned world. I could run through all the classic SF texts in a similar fashion. Philip K Dick, seen by some as the most significant writer of SF in the American postwar tradition, sets his books in a future that almost exactly resembles 1950s American suburbia; Sheri Tepper's *Grass* (1989) takes us to a distant future and a faraway planet in order to tell a story-line about Catholic guilt and fox-hunting.

Let me restate this point with another example. When the television series *Star Trek* was first aired in the late 1960s, it worked hard to produce a design of futuristic living that seemed plausibly of the future. But watching original-series *Star Trek* today is an interesting temporally dislocated experience. It is a show that purports to be set in the twenty-third century, and which includes many things, such as faster-than-light travel, matter-transportation beams and so on, that are more advanced than current technology. In that regard, it is 'futuristic'. But it is also, and at the same time, egregiously dated in a rather quaint and unmistakably 1960s fashion. The clothes worn, the spaces inhabited, even the relative crudity of the special effects, constantly remind us that we are looking backwards not forwards. I remember watching *Star Trek: the Next Generation* when that show was first aired in the 1980s and being struck only by how suave and futuristic it looked. Watching re-runs, I am amazed by how extraordinarily dated and of-its-time it seems. The effect, I think, is to problematise in an interesting way our attitudes towards the temporal component of SF.

According to Fredric Jameson, the older cultural genres have 'spread out and colonised reality itself' (Jameson 1990: 371). This is more true of SF, I think, than any other genre. Just count the number of ways in which we can think about the world today that have been shaped by science fiction. The symbolic purchase of SF on contemporary living is so powerful, and speaks so directly to the realities of our accelerated culture, that it provides many of the conceptual templates of the modern Western world. The complex debates surrounding the genetic engineering of foodstuffs, for instance, enter popular consciousness in SF terms as 'Frankenstein foods'. The dangers of asteroid impact on our world find expression in such SF texts as the films *Deep Impact* (1997) and *Armageddon* (1998). Our feelings about computers have been rehearsed by every SF text that includes artificial intelligence; actual exploration of our solar system seems tame to us because our expectations have been raised by the thrills of SF imagery; many people regard the trope of UFO abductions to be fact rather than science fiction, partly because of the expertness of SF texts such as *The X-Files*. As Istvan Csicsery-Ronay Jr puts it, 'SF has ceased to be a genre per se, becoming instead a mode of awareness about the world' (Csicsery-Ronay 1991: 308). SF does not project us into the future; it relates to us stories about our present, and more importantly about the past that has led to this present.

CASE STUDY: FRANK HERBERT'S *DUNE* (1965)

These various ways of defining SF, as a literature of cognitive estrangement, as a literature of alterity that does not necessarily escape a reductive sense of 'difference' as dangerous, as materialistic symbolism and as a nostalgic, historiographic mode of writing, can all be illustrated via a reading of one of the undisputed masterpieces of 1960s SF, Frank Herbert's large novel *Dune*.

The novel as we have it is divided into three parts: *Dune*, *Muad'Dib* and *The Prophet*, which is a rough index of how Herbert orchestrates his components. Paul Atreides, the hero, comes to Dune as an outsider; he is born on the Earth-like planet Caladan and arrives on Arrakis (Dune) at the age of 16 with his father Duke Leto. This enables the first part of the book to introduce the world and culture of the desert planet, thus arranging our encounter with difference through the device of the initiation of the protagonist. At the end of this first part, the evil Baron Harkonnen seizes the planet and murders Paul's father, forcing Paul to flee. The second part, which takes as its title the name Paul adopts among the Fremen, the desert dwellers, details his Lawrence-of-Arabia-style encounter with the ways of the desert tribes, his acceptance by the Fremen, his adoption of the position of ruler and his taking of a Fremen wife. The third section is where the religious strand takes centre stage. In terms of basic narrative the final third of the book is a return: Paul takes his revenge against Harkonnen and the Emperor and the book comes full circle.

In many senses, then, this is an old-fashioned book. As critic Timothy O'Reilly describes it: 'It is a heroic romance of the best kind. Good and evil are clear-cut. The growth of young Paul to a heroic figure who can snatch victory from overwhelming defeat is a growth in awareness and self-mastery, as well as power. What reader is not heartened when Paul triumphs over all the forces massed against him?' (O'Reilly 1981: 150). And, of course, the whole universe that Herbert creates is almost medieval in terms of its technological non-sophistication. To put it another way, the nostalgic cast of this novel inflects its representation of technology. Herbert's universe is one without much by way of machinery, and with nothing at all by way of thinking machines or computers; these were wiped out in the 'Butlerian jihad', 'the crusade against computers, thinking machines, and conscious robots' (Herbert, *Dune* (1965): 594). Generally speaking, most of the technology in this novel would not be out of place in a shop today. More particularly, there are only two areas in which *Dune* introduces items that we might think of as technological nova, and even these are compromised by the logic of the novel. One is interstellar travel, a necessary precondition for the book we might think; and yet this premise is explained not scientifically but mystically, with the space-ships depending upon pilots who are Spice-addicted (drug-addicted) mutants and therefore no longer human: 'The Guildsman was an elon-gated figure, vaguely humanoid with finned feet and hugely fanned membranous hands ... his tank's vents emitted a pale orange cloud rich with the smell of the geriatric spice, melange' (Herbert 1967: 11). The Spice and the Guildsman's mutated form enable him to somehow sense his path through 'foldspace', the SF-standard hyperspace, and guide a spaceship on its path. We are given no sense of the mechanics or tech-nology of space flight apart from this peculiar quasi-religious staging, and there are no scenes set in space in Dune or the next three of its sequels (*Dune Messiah*, *Children of Dune* and *God Emperor of Dune*). The effect of this is to defamiliarise technology, to characterise it as 'magic' or 'religion' rather than quotidian machinery.

The other technological novum of the novel has to do with weaponry and war. We are introduced to a variety of alarming-sounding weapons in the novel: the 'lasgun', a 'continuous wave laser projector', the 'Maula Pistol' with its poisoned darts, the five-centimetre-long Hunter-Seeker, 'a common assassination weapon that every child of royal blood learned about at an early age. It was a ravening sliver of metal guided by some near-by hand and eye. It could burrow into moving flesh and chew its way up nerve channels to the nearest vital organ' (Herbert, *Dune* (1965): 84). We also learn about Defensive Shields, which can be worn individ-ually or arranged about buildings or whole cities, that 'will permit entry only to objects moving at slow speeds' and that have rendered the use of lasguns almost irrelevant, since a lasgun fired at a shield will result in 'explosive pyrotechnics' powerful enough to destroy both attacker and defender. But at the same time that Herbert is detailing these fancy war technologies, he is undercutting the futuristic burden. An early chapter sees Paul being trained in knife-fighting by the Atreides weapons-mas-ter Gurney Halleck. As with 1977's *Star Wars*, a film which, as several critics have noted, owes a great deal to *Dune*, a fascination with the toy-like ingenuity of machine technology is ultimately undercut by a deeper sense of satisfaction at a retro-defined sense of chivalric conflict. This happens on a personal level, so that the battles in *Dune* are fought by individuals with knives and swords. But it also happens on a larger one: Paul eventually defeats the Emperor and captures the planet by resorting to antique weaponry, namely atomic bombs, that had been long outlawed.

In both these senses, then, *Dune* is a novel built around a sense of stepping backwards; it portrays a world supposedly immensely removed from us in time and space, thousands of light years away and in the year 10,190, but actually intensely familiar to us because of its groundedness in a medieval Arabian paradigm made familiar to us through literature and film (particularly through David Lean's film *Lawrence of Arabia* of 1962). Its familiarity depends upon its old-fashionedness, and the old-fashioned heroic-romance storyline and old-fashioned props only reinforce this. Nor, to be clear about this, am I suggesting that this is entirely a bad thing. It helps explain why *Dune* is so effective. The sense of detail and completeness, of an imagined universe that is larger than the bits that happen to be presented to us in the novel, gives the book a breadth most novels, let alone SF novels, lack; and that sense of verisimilitude in turn depends upon the fact that the book is rooted in actual experience. To mention an example from a parallel mode of writing, Fantasy, J. R. R. Tolkien does something similar in *The Lord of the Rings* by writing a personal and idiosyncratic mythology that is firmly rooted in the actual mythologies of northern Europe.

But this begs certain questions about *Dune* in respect of its encounter with otherness or the alien. A world so familiar, with so little that is radically new to us, could easily be a stale and imaginatively poor world. This situation is made more acute by the way Herbert uses a binarism at least as old as the novel itself to propel his story onwards. What I mean by this is that the motor for this story is a straightforward moral battle, a battle between good and evil. The good is the family Atreides, and Paul in particular, and their 'goodness' is emphasised by a hundred details – they are humane, civilised, cultured, intelligent. When Paul's mother, the Lady Jessica, realises that physician Yueh's wife had been killed by Harkonnen, her reaction is one of instinctive compassion: '"Forgive me," Jessica said. "I do not mean to open an old wound." And she thought Those animals!' (Herbert, *Dune* (1965): 79). In a key scene Duke Leto, flying over the desert to inspect one of his own Spice-mining operations, saves the crew from attack by the ravenous giant sandworms that infest the desert. The ecologist Kynes, watching the bravery and humanity of the action, is impressed despite himself:

> *This Duke was concerned more over the men than he was over the spice. He risked his own life and that of his son to save the men. He passed off the loss of a spice crawler with a gesture. The threat to men's lives had him in a rage. A leader such as that would command fanatical loyalty ...* Against his own will and all previous judgments, Kynes admitted to himself: *I like this Duke.*

> (Herbert, *Dune* (1965): 150)

After the Duke is betrayed and killed, Paul survives by virtue of physical strength and bravery, ingenuity and determination. He is unambiguously heroic.

By way of contrast, the 'evil' half of the moral equation is painted in utterly despicable colours. The villains of the piece come close to caricature. 'Beast' Rabban, with his unspeakable (and unspoken) wickednesses; Feyd-Rautha, who is fond of fighting to the death in – once again – old-fashioned 'Roman Empire' gladiatorial-style combats, but, so as not to risk getting hurt, only ever fights carefully chosen opponents who are drugged beforehand to render them almost helpless; the Padishah Emperor Shaddam IV, a two-dimensional mixture of decadent obsession with the splendour of court and brutally oppressive tyranny, enforced by his SS-like shock troops the Sardaukar. But worst of all is the grotesque figure of Baron Harkonnen, and it is the Baron's overweight body that is the most obvious focus for the limitations of the representation of otherness in *Dune*.

Harkonnen is a very effective villain, but his villainy is a direct function of his otherness. He is, to begin with, foreign: his name ('Vladimir') suggests that he is coded as Russian. As O'Reilly points out, 'the Russian sound' of the Baron's name 'was clearly meant to engage our prejudices, which, it must be remembered, were much stronger when *Dune* was written in the early sixties than they are now' (O'Reilly 1981: 55). He is physically grotesque, enormously fat, so obese that he can only move around with 'suspensors' strapped to his body to carry most of its weight. It is his physical repulsiveness that is most consistently dwelt upon. His first appearance is crudely if effectively orchestrated, as he plots the downfall of the Atreides house in the shadows like a Bond villain: 'a relief globe of the world, partly in shadows, spinning under the impetus of a fat hand that glittered with rings' (Herbert, *Dune* (1965): 25). The point of this goes beyond a class-based characterisation of Harkonnen as 'decadent', although he is that. The response is more visceral. 'As he emerged from the shadows, his figure took on dimension – grossly and immensely fat' (p. 33). But in addition to being coded as repulsive because *racially* and *physically* different from the heroic 'norm' established by Paul, the Baron is also negatively portrayed as *sexually* different. This amounts to a crudely worked-through homophobia. A few pages after presiding over the deaths of Yueh and Piter with utter cold-bloodedness, and after consigning Arrakis to, as he thinks, sixty years of tyranny, Harkonnen is explicitly compared to the Devil, or at least the Beast of Revelation: 'Leto suddenly recalled a thing Gurney Halleck had once said, seeing a picture of the Baron: *And I stood upon the sand of the sea and saw a beast rise out of the sea ... and upon his hands the name of blasphemy*' (p. 213). And at the end of the same chapter, apparently as a means of climactically reinforcing just how repulsive and despicable the Baron is, we discover not only that he is homosexual but that he has lustful designs upon Paul Atreides himself:

'I'll be in my sleeping chambers,' the Baron said. 'Bring me that young fellow we bought on Gamont, the one with the lovely eyes. Drug him well. I don't feel like wrestling.'

'Yes, m'Lord.'

The Baron turned away ... *Yes*, he thought. *The one with the lovely eyes, the one who looks so much like the young Paul Atreides.*

(Herbert, *Dune* (1965): 219)

This may have been less obviously objectionable in the 1960s; today it strikes an odd note. Why should the fact that Harkonnen is gay or that he finds Paul attractive – Paul is certainly presented as being attractive – be in itself a reason to detest him? The point reflects uneasily, I think, on just how old fashioned a novel *Dune* is, how unquestioned its moral schema and therefore its prejudices are. We are given a world of few, if any, moral ambiguities; right is clear cut and wrong signals its presence by being repulsive or effeminate or, indeed, both. Otherness, or 'the alien', is in the first instance represented through the perspective of a tribal culture based on the medieval Bedouin, for whom any person or thing from outside the tribe was to be treated with suspicion and even hatred. This might be thought fatally to compromise the novel's ability to represent the alien. The characters we encounter are, if anything, rather two dimensional, rather ordinary, familiar to us from countless other novels.

But there is one crucial novum in *Dune* which steps outside the restrictive binary of 'good versus evil' in which much of the rest of the novel is trapped: the giant sandworms, the enormous serpent-like alien creatures that are crucial to the ecology of the planet. And here, I think, Herbert does something very clever. He is able to throw the alien into relief against a background of familiarity and therefore make the otherness all the more striking, all the more powerful. This is why the giant sandworms stand out so powerfully in the imagination of the readers of *Dune*.

The sandworms live beneath the surface of the sands of the desert, non-sentient but drawn to the pockets of the drug 'Spice', and to any regular sound made on the surface. Most of the inhabitants of the planet fear these monstrous, alien beasts; but it is a sign of his religious destiny that Paul is able to see past this shallow response. The worm is connected with Paul's acceptance by the Fremen, because he must learn to ride one as they do to become truly one of the tribe. As he faces this test, the otherness of the beast becomes beauty: '*Come up you lovely monster*, he thought. *Up. You hear me calling*' (p. 463). The enormous worms are segmented, and a rider can compel them to stay on the surface of the desert by prising back the edge of one of these segments with a grappling hook; rather than get sand under its skin, the worm will carry the rider over the surface of the desert. Once he succeeds in mounting the worm, Paul revels in his power:

> He felt exultant, like an emperor surveying the world. He suppressed a sudden urge to cavort there, to turn the worm, to show off his mastery of this creature.
>
> (Herbert, *Dune* (1965): 464)

This may be poorly written ('cavort' is an especially ugly touch), but it does at least dramatise the symbolic pertinence of this novum. At the book's climax, the Fremen army ride into battle, and victory, on the backs of the sandworms; Paul turns his empire from dream to reality. In other words, we understand what epistemological riddle the worms stand for, what they stand for symbolically. They represent Power, the power to devour and terrify. They represent man's power over nature in that they are ridden by men; they represent the power of the army as they carry the Fremen troops to victory; and most important of all for the universe Herbert has created, they represent political power on the grand scale, because they are specifically implicated in the creation of Spice, the drug on which all political power rests.

It is the sandworms that dominate *Dune*. They are the most potent and the most memorable of Herbert's inventions in the novel, the thing readers carry away with them. And it seems clear to me that the reason for this is that it is in the figure of the sandworms that Herbert found his most powerful and least flawed embodiment of alterity. The worms are utterly different from us, or from anything we know; and that they are located in a world that is familiar enough from cultural representations of medieval Arabia only serves to highlight the beautiful strangeness of the beasts. They embody alienness in themselves, as well as carrying with them the connotation of the strangeness of the desert landscape that Herbert evokes so well. And more than this, as I have been arguing, they encode the operation of power as itself strange, *not* as natural or ordinary but as outlandish. It is this level of signification that renders *Dune* an effective novel, I think, that underlies all the cruder ethical binarism of good versus evil that otherwise lumpishly separates and condemns alterity in the text. There is, in other words, enough genuine encounter with difference in this novel, particularly the striking sandworms and the intriguing Spice, to carry the text beyond its otherwise disfiguring condemnations of racial, physical and sexual difference. And as a novel it can put together an oblique and suggestive coding of the operation of power as the revaluation of all value, the encounter with otherness.

The mysticism of *Dune* coalesces around gender distinctions. A mystical sect that is exclusively female, the Bene Gesserit Sisterhood, has been operating a breeding policy for thousands of years, hoping to produce a specific individual with tremendous powers of insight into the future and the past. Although this mystic spirituality is something they reserve for women, it seems that this Messiah-figure, called in the novel the Kwisatch Haderach, can only be a man. In other words, potent though the female purchase on these mystical abilities is, there is something a woman lacks that this man has, something that will empower him to do things that a woman cannot do. On a symbolic level, it seems clear that there is some transcendental signifier being alluded to here. As the novel progresses, and it becomes apparent that Paul is indeed the Kwisatch Haderach, his triumphant power-symbolic experience on the unavoidably phallic sandworms takes on the connotations of a particular discourse of gender. This in turn connects the symbolism of this novel to lived experience. Its symbolic nova open up fertile avenues of interpretation that work into the discourses of power and masculinity. The limitations of the novel's ethical schema can be seen in this light as a critique of the narrowness of masculine, phallic power, the anxieties it expresses about male homosexuality being nothing more than the inherent contradictions of the masculinist ideology. SF, according to Peter Lev in *The Cyborg Handbook*, is 'a privileged vehicle for the presentation of ideology. Because it is less concerned than other genres with the surface structure of social reality, science fiction can pay more attention to the deep structures of what is and what ought to be' (Gray *et al.* 1995: 30). *Dune* is a good example of this.

2

THE HISTORY OF SF

Where does science fiction begin? Read the critics of the genre and you can take your pick of possible starting points, for the identification of the point of origin for SF is as fiercely contested a business as defining the form. Different critics have their own favourite jumping-off points. Some go back no further than a hundred years, to H. G. Wells and Jules Verne, giving SF as a genre a youthfulness to fit its supposedly juvenile, forward-fixated profile. Others insist on searching out 'fantastic' or 'science-fictional' elements in literature as ancient as literature is itself. There are journeys to the Moon or heroic protagonists seeking out new worlds and strange new civilisations in the oldest epics of human culture, from the ancient Sumerian *Epic of Gilgamesh* (written perhaps in 2000 BC) onwards. This presents us with two broad approaches to the question of origins, and the difference between these two approaches focuses different ways of understanding the nature of SF. Stress the relative youth of the mode and you are arguing that SF is a specific artistic response to a very particular set of historical and cultural phenomena; more specifically, you are suggesting that SF could only have arisen in a culture experiencing the Industrial Revolution, or one undergoing the metaphysical anxieties of what nineteenth-century philosopher Friedrich Nietzsche called 'the Death of God'. Stress the antiquity of SF, on the other hand, and you are arguing instead that SF is a common factor across a wide range of different histories and cultures, that it speaks to something more durable, perhaps something fundamental in the human make-up, some human desire to imagine worlds other than the one we actually inhabit.

I want, in this chapter, to sketch out three overlapping but different 'histories' of science fiction, giving some indication of what each of them implies for our understanding of the genre. They are: a long history stretching back at least to 1600; a history that takes Mary Shelley's *Frankenstein* (1818) as its starting point and sees SF as a sort of Gothic literature; and a history that begins with American magazine editor Hugo Gernsback (who coined the term 'science fiction' in 1927).

THE LONG HISTORY OF SCIENCE FICTION

The tradition of 'fantasy' is as old as literature and considerably older than the 'realist' fiction that sometimes, impertinently, pretends to be 'mainstream' today. Almost all the oldest and greatest works of human culture contain 'magical' episodes. But if we are interested in the more specifically materialist idiom of the fantastic, then SF begins with a short book by a German astronomer, written probably around 1600 although not published until 1634, Kepler's *Somnium*.

It is hard – indeed, I would argue, impossible – to identify science-fictional texts written before 1600; not because there is any shortage of fantastical or imaginative tales, nor because the focus of literature was purely mundane. On the contrary, there are many prior works that take protagonists to the Moon or further into the solar system. Both Cicero's Latin *Somnium Scipionis* ('The Dream of Scipio', 51 BC) and Plutarch's Greek *to kuklô tês selênês* ('The Circle of the Moon', c. AD 80) site the solar system as a place traversed by virtuous souls after death. Lucian of Samos's *Alêthês Historia* ('The True History', c. AD 170) includes an episode in which a ship is swept into outer space by a great storm and eventually lands on the Moon, which is shown populated by a series of wonderfully grotesque beings. Jumping ahead somewhat, there is the fat epic-romance *Orlando Furioso* ('Mad Roland', 1534) by the Italian poet Ludovico Ariosto, one episode of which takes a character to the Moon on the back of a hippogriff to recover the lost wits of the story, the pleasant conceit of the poem being that everything lost (including sanity) makes its way to the Moon.

The reason why it is distorting to call these works science fiction (although some critics have done so) is not that subsequent science has proven their visions of the cosmos wrong. Science is always proving the visions of SF authors wrong; it was, for instance, a convention of much early twentieth-century SF that beneath the clouds of Venus lay a vast ocean, but the subsequent discovery that in fact Venus is an arid, acidic and superheated planet does not eject those earlier works from the club of SF. The problem with the pre-1600 version of outer space was that it was conceived as a pure and religious realm, a geocentric series of spheres of which only the lowest (ours) was subject to change, and everything above the level of the Moon was incorruptible, eternal and godly. Not until the great Polish astronomer Copernicus (1473–1543) proposed the heliocentric cosmos did a properly materialist understanding of the solar system percolate through to culture more generally.

Johann Kepler (1571–1630) was a Protestant German astronomer who established three important laws of planetary motion. But in addition to his scientific studies, he wrote one work of science fiction, *Somnium, sive Astronomia Lunaris* ('A Dream, or Lunar Astronomy'). This work relates, in a dream, a visit to the Moon, the journey accomplished by being carried there by witches, and provides us with an imaginary natural history of the Moon, or 'Levania' as its natives call it. From a Moon-based point of view, the dominant object in the sky is the Earth, or 'Volva' as the Levanians call it. The Moon's month-long revolution on its own axis and its monthly orbit of the Earth means, of course, that one lunar hemisphere is always facing the Earth and one facing away. The former hemisphere of Levania is called by its inhabitants Subvolva, or 'UnderEarth', and the latter Privolva, or 'deprived-of-Earth'. Kepler correctly deduces that the consequent changes in lunar temperature are extreme, from the great cold of the fortnight-long Levanian night to the great heat of the fortnight-long day; so hot is the lunar day, indeed, that the inhabitants of that world retire into deep caves and caverns to escape it. Life in Privolva, on the other hand, is described in nightmarish terms:

> They live an unfixed life, without permanent habitation. They roam in great crowds over the whole globe during one of their days, some on

> legs which are longer than are our camels', others flying through the
> air, others still in boats follow the fleeing water.
>
> (Kepler, *Somnium*, 46)

The narrative is supported by a series of lengthy scientific notes, exhaustively justifying Kepler's speculations with reference to his scientific observations.

With improved astronomical instruments and a properly scientific understanding of the solar system, seventeenth-century science made great advances in understanding the cosmos, and seventeenth-century science fiction became a vigorous new form of writing. Bishop William Godwin's *The Man in the Moone: or, A Discourse of a Voyage Thither by Domingo Gonsales, the Speedy Messenger* (1638) flies its protagonist moonwards by, rather improbably, having him harness a number of special geese; but once he gets there, the lunar world and occupants are vividly described. John Wilkins's *Discovery of a World in the Moone* (1638) imaginatively extrapolates from scientific data and looks forward to lunar colonies 'as soon as the art of flying is found out'. Savinien Cyrano de Bergerac, in the comical voyage to the Moon in *L'Autre Monde ou les États et Empires dans la lune* ('The Other World, or the States and Empires of the Moon', 1657), invents a sort of rocket, flies to the Moon and encounters a series of weird and wonderful creatures, who (for instance) use music instead of words as language, and who inhale their food instead of eating it. If we can go there, then perhaps they could come here. French novelist Charles Sorel's *La Vraie Histoire Comique de Francion* ('The True Comic History of Francion', 1626) has his protagonist look up at the Moon in alarm, wondering whether 'there's a prince like Alexander the Great up there, planning to come down and subdue this world of ours. He'll need to provide engines for descending to our world ...' (Sorel, *Vraie Histoire*, 425).

By the eighteenth century this vigorous sub-genre of interplanetary adventures had spread out and become a major feature of European literature. Romances were being published all over Europe taking characters on adventures into the solar system (for instance, Eberhard Christian Kindermann's novel *Die geschwinde Reise auf dem Luft-Schiff nach der Oberen Welt, welche jüngsthin fünf Personen angestellt* ('The rapid journey by airship to the upper world, recently taken by five people', 1744) records a journey to Mars by balloon) or having aliens come to visit us (Voltaire's *Micromégas*, 'Littlebig', of 1750 imagines aliens of prodigious size from Sirius and Jupiter scrutinising the inhabitants of the Earth) or taking the adventure into an imaginary kingdom located within the Earth (in Ludvig Holberg's *Nikolai Klimi iter subterraneum*, 'Nikolai Klim's Journey beneath the Earth', 1741, the protagonist falls into the hollow space within the Earth and discovers a central mini-sun and a mini-system of planets). Many utopias – voyages to imaginary lands where society functions much better than in the real world, a genre named after Thomas More's early Latin fantasia *Utopia* (1516) – and speculations about possible futures were also written. A book such as Jonathan Swift's *Gulliver's Travels* (1726) uses its peripatetic protagonist as a means of visiting a range of fantastic and utopian earthly societies (the diminutive Lilliputians or the gigantic Brobdignagians) as well as satirically extrapolating eighteenth-century science into a properly speculative and science-fictional realm; in the third section of the novel Gulliver is taken aboard a floating city, kept aloft by a powerful magnetic device, and meets scientists whose speculations about the cosmos have alienated them from real life.

I could list several hundred science-fictional works from the seventeenth and eighteenth centuries, but in many ways the interesting thing about them for our purposes is precisely that so few critics of SF are prepared to include them in their histories of the genre. In part this is because these works, which read as archaic according to the contemporary-fascinated aesthetics of many readers of SF, are just not to the taste of many people. Some critics who read twentieth-century SF with pleasure can only read a work such as Marie-Anne de Roumier's *Les Voyages de Milord Ceton dans les sept Planettes* ('The Voyages of Lord Ceton in the Seven Planets', 1765) dutifully, as a period piece; and it is always easier to write critically about books one actually likes. And there's more to this than merely a kind of blinkered denial of pedigree. To talk in a meaningful way of the 'science fictional megatext' (and any history of SF is, in fact, a chronological delineation of that megatext) must mean to talk of constituent texts that possess cultural resonance. A book such as H. G. Wells's *War of the Worlds* (1898) is still being read today, still inspiring movie versions and other adaptations, still influencing new writers working on the theme of alien invasion; this is what gives it a crucial place in the megatext. A work such as Marie-Anne de Roumier's is, simply, not (for better or worse). Archivists and academics may insist that the long history of science fiction is the most complete, but if we are interested in SF as a presently vibrant cultural fact, then only those texts still 'alive' in some sense should be included; and the earliest such text is probably Mary Shelley's short novel *Frankenstein* (1818).

THE GOTHIC HISTORY OF SF

According to come critics, modern SF was born out of, and presently has much in common with, the sub-genre of 'Gothic fiction'. As author and critic Brian Aldiss argues: 'Science fiction was born from the Gothic mode, is hardly free of it now. Nor is the distance between the two modes great. The Gothic emphasis was on the distant and the unearthly' (Aldiss 1973: 18).

The critic M. H. Abrams lists the conventions frequently found in the Gothic, a mode frequently set 'in a gloomy castle replete with dungeons, subterranean passages, and sliding panels' which 'made bountiful use of ghosts, mysterious disappearances and other sensational and supernatural occurrences ... their principal aim was to evoke chilling terror' (Abrams 1985: 74). But the Gothic was only a symptom of the larger literary and cultural phenomenon known as 'Romanticism', and in particular it is the primacy of notions of the Imagination and the Sublime associated with Romantic writing that sets the agenda for the development of SF. Not only Romantic poets like William Blake and Percy Bysshe Shelley, but also writers of Gothic novels like Horace Walpole and Mary Shelley, foregrounded 'the Imagination' as the key artistic faculty. And it was the deployment of Imagination, which we can read for our purposes as 'the creative entering into the possibilities of the fantastic, the unknown and the other-than-the-everyday', together with the awe-inspiring splendour of 'the Sublime', which today is behind what is sometimes called 'Sense of Wonder SF', that established the artistic framework within which all modern SF writers work.

Specifically, it is commonly asserted that, in Paul Alkon's words, 'science fiction starts with Mary Shelley's *Frankenstein*' (Alkon 1994, 1). This often gnashingly written fable about an ambitious scientist who creates an artificial creature, unnamed and described throughout as 'the monster', which being is abandoned by its creator and becomes a destructive force, retains its potency today. It has been so often reimagined and envisioned, particularly in the cinema, that most people have some sense of the core of the story. To return to the novel itself can even be a slightly disorienting experience; Patrick Parrinder justly calls it 'an immature work which nevertheless has been enormously influential' (Parrinder 1979: 11). But the secret of *Frankenstein*'s success is not hard to divine. It is in the detailed manifestation of the beautiful strangeness of the monster that the book strikes home; it is, in other words, the way its central character, who is also its novum, functions as an embodiment of alterity. The strategies Shelley uses to this end are various. Most obviously there is the sheer novelty of the creature's origins, 'manufactured' by a scientist. In a later preface Shelley first added the suggestion that electricity may have played some part in animating the thing; in the novel as we have it there are no details as to how this feat was achieved. Along similar lines, the extremities of experience in the novel, the extreme violence, the extreme fear, are Gothic attempts at sublimity, at articulating a state of being other than the ordinary. The polar landscapes of the novel's conclusion are the apotheosis of this. The narrator encounters both Frankenstein and his 'monstrous' creation in an environment as far removed from the sorts of environment we are used to as it is possible to find on the surface of this planet. This symphony of Gothic difference produces some of the novel's most overwrought passages. Frankenstein pursues his monster over the polar ice-cap, a land that metaphorically reproduces the alienated strangeness of the novel's central conceit: 'Oh!' the narrator declares, 'how unlike it was to the blue seasons of the south!' (p. 199). Frankenstein almost apprehends him, but the elements intervene.

> But now, when I appeared almost within grasp of my foe ... the wind arose; the sea roared; and, as with the mighty shock of an earthquake, it split, and cracked with a tremendous and overwhelming sound ... in a few minutes a tumultuous sea rolled between me and my enemy, and I was left drifting on a scattered piece of ice.
>
> (Mary Shelley, *Frankenstein* (1992): 201)

This sort of writing is clumsy, maybe, but it does possess a certain urgent vividness. A passage like this symbolically apprehends the themes of the novel, what Aldiss calls 'the disintegration of society which follows man's arrogation of power. We see one perversion of the natural order leading to another' (Aldiss 1973: 27). Shelley's novum, the alienated monster, articulates the way 'science' cuts itself off from the more organic processes of nature, and in turn functions as a symbol for a modern sense of alienated existence. Darko Suvin argues that *Frankenstein* sets in motion a recurrent theme of SF, the idea that 'progress becomes indissoluble from catastrophe' (Suvin 1979: 10).

Important though Shelley's novel has been in the development of SF, it is not until the end of the nineteenth century, and the work of Verne and Wells, that we start to see the actual growth of SF as a meaningful category in its own right, which is to say as something more than the occasional single novel. And it is through Wells, rather than Verne, that fiction centrally concerned with the encounter with difference is most thoroughly developed. But, for both writers, Gothic tropes and a Gothic mood often define their manner of SF.

Jules Verne (1828–1905) was particularly adept at stories of fantastic voyages. *Voyage au centre de la terre* ('Voyage to the Centre of the Earth', 1864) follows its protagonists down the shaft of an extinct Icelandic volcano into the hollow space at the Earth's core; its narrative and descriptive evocations of the sublime give it an imaginative potency. In particular, Verne's vision of enormous subterranean caverns filled with primal oceans containing dinosaur monsters functions as an effective symbol of the same unconscious arena represented by so many Gothic cellars, dungeons and caves. Other works by Verne are grounded in a particular, rationalist perspective on the virtues of technology. We see this in the much-filmed *20,000 lieues sous les mers* ('Twenty Thousand Leagues under the Sea', 1872), with its high-tech (for the 1870s) submarine, the 'Nautilus'; or the interplanetary *De la terre à la lune* ('From the Earth to the Moon', 1865), in which the protagonists' spaceship achieves escape velocity by being fired from an enormous cannon. All Verne's books are set in a version of his present day, and when he invented such SF props as a spaceship, he was keen to work them from existing scientific principles. The principle of lunar exploration outlined in *De la terre à la lune* may seem outlandish to us (after all, firing astronauts from a cannon would surely squash them dead), but Verne thought it preferable to the sorts of device imagined by his contemporaries. H. G. Wells also wrote a story about lunar exploration, *The First Men in the Moon* (1901), in which a scientist invents a metal that denies gravity; he constructs a sphere of this material, inside which he and a friend are able to float off the face of the Earth and to the Moon. Verne was not impressed and commented on Wells's novel, getting the details wrong to be doubly disdainful:

> I make use of physics. He invents. I go to the moon in a cannon-ball, discharged from a cannon. Here there is no invention. He goes to Mars in an airship, which he constructs of a material which does away with the laws of gravitation. *Ça c'est très joli* [that's all very well] ... but show me this metal. Let him produce it.
>
> (Verne, quoted in Parrinder 1980: 7)

The effect, in Verne's fiction, is, as John Clute puts it, 'a sense of coming very close to but never toppling over the edge of the known' (Clute and Nicholls 1993: 1276). There is, in other words, a certain limitation to the Verneian encounter with difference.

H. G. Wells (1866–1946) is, as the critic Patrick Parrinder has put it, 'the pivotal figure in the evolution of scientific romance into modern science fiction. His example has done as much to shape SF as any other single literary influence' (Parrinder 1980: 10). Parrinder thinks this has to do with Wells's skill in generic combination, added to the fact that he mastered a range of 'representative themes (time-travel, the alien invasion, biological mutation, the future-city, the anti-utopia)'. But behind all of this is a Wellsian fascination with encountering difference embodied in material form, and a lucid sense of the symbolic possibilities of the imaginative novum. Nearly all his early stories concern men meeting strange life forms; for instance 'The Stolen Bacillus', 'In the Avu Observatory', 'The Flowering of the Strange Orchid' and 'Aepyornis Island', all of which were published in 1894. His early short novel *The Island of Doctor Moreau* (1896) is a powerful reworking of *Frankenstein*, and through Shelley a revisioning of Milton's *Paradise Lost*. Wells's scientist, the vivisectionist Moreau, has sequestered himself on a tropical island, where he has been surgically reworking various animals, making their physiques more human and enhancing their brains. These creations are 'monstrous' in much the way that Shelley's monster was; which is to say, they are both repulsive and also oddly attractive, beautifully strange. They have developed a primitive religion, centred on Moreau as a combined God of Mercy and Pain; they chant 'His is the Hand that wounds, His is the Hand that heals'. The novel's Gothic Eden also includes a version of the biblical 'Tree of the Knowledge of Good and Evil' in Moreau's injunction to the beast-men not to taste blood. This command is, of course, transgressed, and the beast-men revert to their bestial origins. All this provides Wells with a straightforward vehicle for satirising religion. But it is the variety of beast-men themselves, based on dogs, pumas, pigs, monkeys – 'they wore turbans too, and thereunder peered out their elfin faces at me, faces with protruding lower jaws and bright eyes' (Wells, *The Science Fiction*, Vol. 1 (1995): 96) – and others that stick in the imagination. As a novum they enable Wells to write fluently about the balance between civilisation and bestiality in humankind. Aldiss considers William Golding's *Lord of the Flies* and George Orwell's *Animal Farm* to be 'this novel's descendants' (Aldiss 1973: 122), but the advantage in embodying the story in a science-fictional idiom is that the connection between bestialism and humanity is established in the logic of the text via exactly the discourse of scientific rationalism that the novel goes on to deconstruct, rather than conceptualising it in naturalistic terms, like Golding, or as fable, like Orwell.

Wells's most famous novel of the encounter with difference, indeed one of the most famous SF novels of all, is *The War of the Worlds* (1898). One of the reasons this novel has had such a lasting impact on the traditions of science fiction has to do with the way Wells is able to work his material into a sort of wrought, mournful beauty, something akin to poetry. He takes a perfectly ordinary man, an especially ordinary place, Woking, and then he imagines the extraordinary erupting into it, in the form of a giant cylinder crashing to Earth from Mars. Tentacled Martians climb out of this cylinder to make war upon humanity from towering mechanical tripods, laying waste to South-east England before eventually succumbing to earthly bacteria against which they have no natural defence. But all this is rendered that much more effective by Wells's impeccable sense of the interlinked beauties of the familiar and the strange. The early chapters of the book build an understated but brilliant sense of anticipation by stressing that very ordinariness.

> There were lights in the upper windows of the houses as the people went to bed. From the railway station in the distance came the sound of shunting trains, ringing and rumbling, softened almost to melody by the distance ... It seemed so safe and tranquil.
>
> (Wells, *The Science Fiction*, Vol. 1 (1995): 189)

The same sort of poetry that Wells can find in the evening shuntings of trains at Woking is repeated in the desolate beauty he evokes in a London emptied by the Martian threat and overrun with the red weed they have brought across space. At this point in the book the last Martian is ceasing its weird cry and dying.

> Abruptly as I crossed the bridge, the sound of 'Ulla, ulla, ulla, ulla' ceased. It was, as it were, cut off. The silence came like a thunderclap.
>
> The dusky houses about me stood faint and tall and dim; the trees towards the park were growing black. All about me the red weed clambered among the ruins, writhing to get above me in the dimness. Night, the mother of fear and mystery, was coming upon me. But while that voice sounded the solitude, the desolation, had been endurable; by virtue of it, London had still seemed alive, and the sense of life about me had upheld me. Then suddenly a change, the passing of something – I knew not what – and then a stillness that could be felt.
>
> (Wells, *The Science Fiction*, Vol. 1 (1995): 309–10)

It is less the specifics of finding a beautiful strangeness in this scenario and more the ways in which it parallels the scenes of calm before the war; it is Wells's dialectical sense of the interrelationship between sameness and otherness that gives this work much of its potency: the cognitive estrangement, in other words.

Wells's potently imagined nova in *The War of the Worlds* symbolically distil the concerns of the age. His Martians are imperialists who use their superior technology to invade a nation, England, which had been accumulating its own empire in part because of a superior technological sophistication. In other words, the arrival of the Martians and their mechanised brutalities are the symbolic forms Wells chose to explore a deeper set of concerns: concerns about the British, rather than the Martian, Empire, about the violence of empire-building, and about the anxieties of otherness and the encounter with otherness that empire imposes on the imperial peoples. Aldiss suggests that Wells's novel 'showed the Imperialist European powers of the day how it felt to be on the receiving end of an invasion armed with superior technology' (Aldiss 1973: 71), but in fact the text is not as straightforwardly turn-about as that. Wells actually inhabits a subtly balanced position between expressing concern about the morality of European imperialism in coded form and reinforcing exactly the ideological underpinnings of that imperialism with a scare story about how easily a ruthless, racially distinct military threat might destroy an underprepared Britain. More specifically, there is something 'Eastern' about Wells's conception of his Martians, from their pseudo-Arabic cry of 'Ulla', like the Islamic cry of 'Allah', to their towering mechanical tripods striding about on metal legs which may derive from Russian folklore of a house that moves about on gigantic chicken legs. In other words, the deftness of Wells's conception is that he is able simultaneously to critique the European imperial excesses, whilst also coding the 'Eastern' threat against which European imperialism specifically justified itself. Suvin captures something of this ideological ambiguity by invoking the name of Nazi propagandist and anti-Semite Joseph Goebbels.

> The Martians from *The War of the Worlds* are described in Goebbelsian terms of repugnantly slimy and horrible 'racial' otherness and given the sole function of bloodthirsty predators (a function that fuses genocidal fire-power – itself described as an echo of the treatment meted out by the imperialist powers to colonized peoples – with the bloodsucking vampirism of horror fantasies).
>
> (Suvin 1979: 78)

The effectiveness of a novel like *The War of the Worlds*, in other words, depends partly upon the sophistication of its balancing of familiar representation and the strangeness of its novum; but that novum also relates symbolically back to key concerns of the society and culture out of which it was produced. It is not a narrow mapping of imperialist anxieties on to a symbolic form, but rather a complex symbolic meditation on the paradoxes of imperialist ideology.

Following on from this, we can argue that SF as a distinctive genre comes to cultural prominence in the Age of Empires precisely because it is a necessary part of the official ideology of empire-forming that difference needs to be flattened, or even eradicated. SF, in other words, figures as the expression of the subconscious aspect of this official ideology. Under the nineteenth-century British Empire the pressure is to conform upwards to a certain model of 'civilised' behaviour. We can see something similar today, under what can more loosely be called the twentieth-century American Empire, where culture treats everybody in the world, whatever their actual identity, as a 'sort-of American'. A film such as *Independence Day* (1997), for instance, figures a world catastrophe as an American catastrophe, with other nations represented in cameo as acquiescing under American leadership and sharing American values. The world, in that film, is America. Similarly, *Star Trek* postulates a 'Federation of Planets' encompassing a wide range of alien worlds, but none the less manages to flatten difference into a kind of Galactic Americana. The 'USS' in *USS Enterprise* stands for 'United Space Ship', but by no coincidence it is also the present-day abbreviation for 'United States Ship'. It is not just a question of American actors filling almost every role, which, of course, we might expect in a show filmed in Los Angeles, but of a representative cultural identity which is Western, bourgeois, family-centred, aspirational, rational, centrally concerned with 'freedom' as the freedom of individualist enterprise: American, in short. I like Star Trek a great deal, but its success as a series depends, it seems to me, on the ways in which it is subtly able to undercut the conformist ideological message that it tends to share with other world-winning American cultural productions. A scene in Nicholas Meyer's film *Star Trek 6: the Undiscovered Country* (1991), where the Klingons quote Shakespeare 'in the original Klingon', is an example of this, wittily inviting us to rethink our assumptions about the 'Western' cultural dominance. In the film the Klingons criticise the Federation as 'a humans-only club', foregrounding the cultural essentialism behind much of the original series.

One of the ways, then, in which an empire establishes itself, justifies itself and continues is by putting out the cultural message that the dominant culture in that empire is best, and that therefore other cultures should conform to it. It does that on the one hand by raising up the values of the dominant culture, and on the other by attacking those who are not part of that culture. In other words, it is involved in praising the Same and demonising the other. That other might be many things: history has given us the other as Jew, as Black, as Arab, as East Asian ('the Yellow Peril'), and as Woman. On the other hand, history's verdict on the Same has been remarkably consistent: the Same has tended to be male, white, Western and associated with military power and technology.

This is, it goes without saying, a crude and brief account of a complex set of cultural and historical circumstances. But my point is that science fiction first emerges as the underside to this set of cultural dominants, as, in a sense, the dark subconscious to the thinking mind of imperialism. Where much mainstream Victorian culture, for instance, is about the patent rightness and decency of 'civilisation' as it was then conceived, science fiction explores the problematics of that term. According to this sort of model, much science fiction can be keyed into cultural and historical specifics. It is no coincidence, the argument would go, that British science fiction experienced a burst of inventive creativity at around the time of Wells, Bram Stoker (1847–1912), Olaf Stapleton (1886–1950) and Rider Haggard (1856–1925), because this period saw the high summer of the British imperial adventure. Similarly, the rise to world domination of the USA after the Second World War saw a cognate flourishing in American SF, the so-called 'Golden Age' of science fiction, leading through the 1950s and 1960s both to SF texts that articulated imperial anxiety (for instance, *Invasion of the Body Snatchers*, 1956) but also to works (such as the ongoing *Star Trek* series) that are all about exploring the new frontier, transferring the colonisation of the American continent directly onto the galaxy.

THE GERNSBACKIAN HISTORY OF SF

A third, related history of the genre locates it more specifically in the twentieth century. The phrase 'science fiction' is first used in the 1920s, and for some critics it is that era that sees the first 'real' SF. Both Verne and Wells were writing deliberately popular fiction and working within the traditions of popular publishing of their day; so it is that Wells's writing grew out of his speculative, mass-market journalism, whilst Verne struck up a lucrative deal with a publisher called Jules Hetzel, who marketed the novels under the popularising rubric of 'voyages extraordinaires'. In America the popular market also dictated the beginnings of SF as a serious genre.

In particular, this is connected with the cheap magazine format known as 'Pulp'. Advances in the manufacture of paper out of woodpulp in the 1880s fuelled a boom in cheap publishing, and a wide range of magazines grew up, printed on a cheap, thick paper that shreds easily and yellows quickly. These soon began catering for specific markets, such as westerns, detective fiction and romantic love stories. The first Pulp to specialise in what we might think of as SF was *Thrill Book*, which started publishing in 1919 and went out of business the same year. The first magazine with any commercial durability was *Amazing Stories*, which began publication in 1926. *Amazing* was founded by Luxembourg-born Hugo Gernsback, who worked hard to define the nascent field of SF. Indeed, according to one influential critic of the genre, although there was 'a prelude to the idea' of SF in the nineteenth century, 'the first true critic of science fiction was Hugo Gernsback', who 'made science fiction a recognized literary form' (Westfahl 1998: 1). In an editorial from 1929 Gernsback talked ambitiously about the term he also claimed to have invented.

> Not only is science fiction an idea of tremendous import, but it is to be an important factor in making the world a better place to live in, through educating the public to the possibilities of science and the influence of science on life ... If every man, woman, boy and girl could be induced to read science fiction right along, there would certainly be a great resulting benefit to the community ... Science fiction would make people happier, give them a broader understanding of the world, make them more tolerant.
>
> (Gernsback, quoted in James 1994: 8–9)

Gernsback used his editorial power to shape the development of the genre, with a strong preference for SF that was grounded thoroughly in science, that was 'educational' almost to the point of being openly didactic. John W. Campbell, the other great name from SF magazine editorship, who took over the rival publication *Astounding Science-Fiction* in 1937, shared this belief that SF should educate as it entertained, and that it should be grounded in science and the celebration of science. At the same time, Campbell insisted of all his contributors that the science should be properly integrated into the story, that there should be no undigested scientific lectures dropped into the text. More than Gernsback, Campbell believed that SF should be about more than just machines and ideas, that the focus should rather be on the ways people responded to and were shaped by those ideas.

However noble these ideas sound, it cannot be denied that the 'Pulps' have a reputation for a very different sort of fiction: for kinetic, fast-paced and exciting tales that are also clumsily written, hurried in conception and morally crude. The critics Clute and Nicholls cite a nicely representative blurb from a 1931 edition of *Astounding*, concerning a story entitled 'The Pirate Planet' by Charles W. Diffin: 'From Earth & Sub-Venus Converge a Titanic Offensive of Justice on the Unspeakable Man-Things of Torg' (Clute and Nicholls 1993: 63). Unspeakable Man-Things – demonisations of otherness, in other words – and their analogues also characterised the look of the Pulps; their brightly coloured, crudely realised cover art was as much part of the effect of the text as the writing inside, representing, for example, men in spacesuits and women in less complete clothing being menaced by insectoid, ape-like or otherwise monstrous aliens. As the critic Edward James put it, 'the American Pulps may have bequeathed a largely unfortunate heritage to SF in the second half of the twentieth century'. James deplores 'their concentration on action not thought, on power rather than responsibility, on aggression not introspection, on wish fulfilment not reality', and goes on to quote Thomas Disch's mournful judgement, from his article 'The Embarrassments of Science Fiction', that 'by far the great part of pulp fiction from the time of Wells till now was written to provide a semi-literate audience with compensatory fantasies' (James 1994: 48).

One of the less-defensible aspects of this was the repeated use of a Wellsian trope of alien invasion in order to celebrate the superiority of humankind over the unprovoked threat from an unspeakable alien menace. This is evident in works such as Edgar Rice Burroughs' *The Moon Maid* (1926) or the comic-strip *Buck Rogers in the 25th Century*, which first appeared in 1929 and was based by Philip Nowlan on his novel *Armageddon 2419*, which in turn had appeared in *Amazing* during 1928–9. In the original incarnation of this adventure Buck Rogers, sent 500 years into the future, discovers that America has been overrun by the evil hordes of 'Red Mongols' and immediately sets-to to battle against the menace. One of the imitators of this successful strip, *Flash Gordon*, which first appeared as a comic strip in 1934, makes the 'orientalism' of the concept more explicit with its Chinese-style villain, the embodiment of all that is evil, the Emperor Ming the Merciless of the Planet Mongo. This coding of invasion paranoia was sometimes even more direct; Heinlein's 1941 novel *Sixth Column*, which first appeared in *Astounding*, is specifically about an Asian invasion of the USA. In each of these cases, SF is being used to reinforce a particular, narrow ideological construction of 'American-ness' by demonising some notional scapegoat.

But sometimes the energy and sprawling inventiveness of the Pulps produced more interesting, viable SF. Two authors particularly associated with the Pulps have endured, partly because they were able to fashion something lastingly strange from the materials of the rapidly solidifying genre in which they worked. Edgar Rice Burroughs (1875–1950) was a prolific and inventive writer, who is probably best remembered today for inventing Tarzan, Lord of the Jungle. More relevant, for our purposes, is his sequence of eleven Mars novels, sometimes called the Barsoom sequence, after the name the natives of Mars give their own planet. The first of these, *A Princess of Mars*, first appeared as early as 1912, in *All-Story Magazine*, but Burroughs was still writing them in the 1940s. His hero is as all-American as Buck Rogers or Flash Gordon, although there is an element of myth, or even mysticism, in Burroughs' conception that tends to unravel the harder-edged SF aspects. Carter, a warrior, does not travel to Mars in a spaceship but effectively by praying to his 'god', Mars, and finding himself simply transported there. Once there he battles against aliens with many arms and various coloured skins (blue, black, green); but he also marries a Martian Princess who is beautiful despite being – or, arguably, *because* she is – red-skinned and egg-laying. It is hard to deny the racism and sexism that underlie much of Burroughs' works of fiction, but there is also enough which is strange in them to unsettle the fixed notions of that sort of bigotry. Most of the fighting is with swords, even though there are various nova on Barsoom that are more advanced, such as radium pistols and antigravity fliers. As we saw with *Dune*, the combination of technological advance and retrostyled old-fashionedness focuses the nostalgic cast of the mode. Burroughs' Barsoom is a backward-looking civilisation, a world that is dying, with a decaying population and drying oceans; its various nova in fact externalise an American perspective on the East not dissimilar to the cruder, morally coloured demonisations of the Orient mentioned above.

E. E. 'Doc' Smith (1890–1965) was an equally prolific Pulp author. It is symptomatic of Gernsback's attempts to dignify the newly coined term 'science fiction' with scientific respectability that he insisted on adding 'PhD' to Smith's name for his contributions to *Amazing*; in fact, Smith had earned his doctorate for his contributions to food science and specialised in doughnut batter. But the *Lensman* novels for which Smith is most famous are distinguished less by a Gernsbackian adherence to the protocols of science and more by a muscular and colourful imaginative fictionalising, a Scholesian 'fabulation'. Effectively, he invented that sub-genre known as 'Space Opera'. Smith shares with Burroughs a fundamental 'good versus evil' vision of the universe in the *Lensman* books, beginning with *Triplanetary* in 1934 and including half a dozen titles that picture a universe divided between the alien embodiments of Good, the Arisians, and the epitomes of Evil, the Eddorians. In terms of the representation of difference, this is not a conception that allows for much subtlety. The Arisians are humanoid, but the Eddorians are shaped as revoltingly different from mankind.

> Arisia was Earth-like … Eddore was and is large and dense; its liquid a poisonous, sludgy syrup; its atmosphere a foul and corrosive fog … Each Eddorian changed, not only its shape, but also its texture, in accordance with the requirements of the moment. Each produced – extruded – members whenever it needed them … filaments or cables; fingers or feet; needles or mauls.
>
> (Smith, *Triplanetary* (1997): 2–4)

These dubious shape-shifting aliens operate behind the scenes of the galaxy, hidden but manipulating it towards its doom. The Arisians, on the other hand, have been breeding human beings to the stage that, with the series protagonist Kim Kinnison, they can take on the minions of the Eddorians and defeat them. The Eddorians, in addition to being physically repulsive and morally evil, are utterly single-minded. In place of the diversity that is central to Smith's notion of 'Civilisation', 'each and every Eddorian' had only one goal: 'power. *Power*! P-O-W-E-R!!' (p. 5). This does not represent a particularly high level of analysis.

Where Smith's novels manage to overcome these limitations is in the sheer size and scope of his imaginative conception. It is hard to think of any SF novels as enamoured of enormity as the *Lensman* books, or Smith's other major sequence of novels, the *Skylark* series. Spaceships are enormous and become more and more vast as Smith's career progresses. There may be a certain quaintness about the description in earlier novels: the *Fearless*, for instance, 'the British super-dread-nought, which was to be the flagship of the fleet – the mightiest and heaviest spaceship which had yet lifted her stupendous mass into the ether' (*Triplanetary*, p. 171). But when reading through Smith's novels in sequence, the proliferation of superlatives of size – 'enormous', 'vast', 'awful', 'colossal', 'mighty', 'stupendous', 'immense' and so on – does batter one's reading sensibilities into a sort of apprehension of awe. Smith's imaginative conception crosses huge stretches of time and space and deploys monumental artefacts. He originally conceived the *Lensman* books as one suitably titanic single novel, 400,000 words in length. Only in the immensity of space, it could be argued, would Smith be able to find a proper correlative for the ambition of his imaginative conception.

Behind this commitment to an aesthetic of scale is a form of elitism that justifies the fan in the belief that SF is a superior genre to conventional literatures precisely because it encompasses grander and more significant vistas. Smith himself, in 1940, asserted that:

> The casual reader does not understand science fiction, does not have sufficient imagination or depth or breadth of vision to grasp it, and hence does not like it ... We science [fiction fans] are imaginative, with a tempered, analytical imaginativeness which fairy tales will not

satisfy. We are critical. We are fastidious. We have a mental grasp and scope.

(Smith, quoted in Huntington 1989: 48)

This amounts to a definition of SF similar to that of Darko Suvin or Robert Scholes, as blending 'imaginative fabulation' and 'cognitive rigour'; but the unashamed rhetoric of superiority makes clear that the novum of cosmic scale does nothing less than map on to a belief in the cognate scale and range of the SF fan's mental faculties.

THE GOLDEN AGE: ASIMOV

There was, then, a great deal of limited SF produced in America before the Second World War, but at the same time there were occasional successes and, more importantly, a framework was laid in which the representation of a radical alterity could be explored. As American fortunes grew, this especially American mode of literature took on some of the energy and ebullience of its national outlook.

Fans talk unironically of 'the Golden Age' in SF, and they usually mean something quite specific: stories published in the late 1930s and 1940s or sometimes, even more specifically, American Pulp publishing in the period 1938–46. This is a short period of time, but it includes a striking wealth and diversity of writing talents: Isaac Asimov, Clifford Simak, Jack Williamson, L. Sprague De Camp, Theodore Sturgeon, Robert Heinlein and A. E. Van Vogt, to name only the shortest list that might be drawn up. The energy and self-confidence of practitioners and fans of SF during this period were extraordinary. In 1948 John W. Campbell, the enormously influential editor of the SF magazine *Astounding*, could talk about SF as something larger than literature.

That group of writings which is usually referred to as 'mainstream literature' is actually a special subgroup of the field of science fiction – for science fiction deals with all places in the Universe, and all times in Eternity, so the literature of the here-and-now is, truly, a subset of science fiction.

(Campbell, quoted in James 1994: 57)

The rhetoric, which resembles the Smith quotation at the end of the previous section in its expansive optimism about the inherent value of the form, is symbolically imperial in so far as it sees SF colonising the entire territory of literature, making the mainstream a subsidiary kingdom.

To concentrate on one of the names from this Golden Age, Isaac Asimov, is to draw out the parallels between Golden Age writing and the Pulp writing that preceded it. To many, it would be a sort of critical sacrilege to suggest that E. E. 'Doc' Smith, popular though he is, can be equated with Asimov. Smith was a hack SF writer who managed some fairly impressive effects, whereas, in the words of C. N. Manlove, 'for many readers of science fiction, Isaac Asimov is the presiding genius of the genre, the old master who revolutionised the form and provided the basis for many of its present characteristics' (Manlove 1986: 15). None the less, in a work such as Asimov's highly regarded and much-imitated *Foundation* series we see a fundamentally Smithesque imaginative process at work.

Asimov's *Foundation* books are set at the close of a Galactic Empire. A scientist (Asimov calls him a 'psychohistorian') called Hari Seldon has analysed with mathematical exactness the way that history works. He can, according to Asimov's conception, do this for the history of a million people to the extent of precisely anticipating the future, although with individuals there are too many variables to enable him to do this. He foresees the downfall of the Empire and the ten thousand years of chaos that will follow. So he sets up his Foundation, ostensibly a group which is compiling the *Encyclopedia Galactica* but which is actually working to preserve and rebuild civilisation, in order to bring society back to normal in a tenth of the time. The novels chart the exact success of Sheldon's prophecies, until a mutant individual called 'the Mule' (so-called because he is sterile) is born. Sheldon could predict the mass dynamics of society but had no way of knowing what freak individuals might arise. As it is, the Mule smashes the Foundation's carefully constructed new civilisation in a drive for power and is only stopped by a mysterious 'Second Foundation' established by Sheldon to step into the breach should the First Foundation fail.

The Mule is the only random element in Asimov's conception of the future, and even that dramatic device was pressed on him by John Campbell. There is something almost comforting in the central

conception, though: that history itself may be completely compre-
hended and therefore controlled. In terms of the encounter with difference, this is the flaw in the work. It transpires that nothing unexpected
can happen in Asimov's universe: even the unexpected – the Mule – was
expected after all, and Sheldon had prepared for this eventuality with a
secretive, hidden organisation, the so-called Second Foundation. Indeed,
where at the beginning of the work we assume that Sheldon's plan was
simply to ease humankind over the break-up of the Galactic Empire, by
the time the Second Foundation is revealed we realise that his conception was grander: to put an end to historical flux altogether. That there
is a slightly sinister edge to this seems difficult to doubt: not only that
these novels set themselves at loggerheads with the randomness of
diversity, but that they embody within themselves precisely that aesthetic of the Same. Colin Manlove talks about the controlled aesthetic
monotony of the conception of these novels: 'persons are usually seen as
typical rather than special, even as clichés ... we do not know how one
planet differs from another ... nor are we given details of battles, linger-
ing accounts of love, different customs of civilisations. There are no animals, only man ... Thought-processes and conversations largely fill the
trilogy, and nearly all these are confined to finding things out and with
gaining power' (Manlove 1986: 28–9).

Frank Herbert's *Dune* novels are often seen as an attempt to rewrite
Asimov's great epic in terms that might take account of the necessary
randomness of historical process, to reconfigure them, in other words, so
as to take more account of difference. There's an elitism behind
Asimov's novels that grates. Indeed, Herbert has commented upon
Asimov's *Foundation* books in exactly these terms.

> History [in the *Foundation* books] ... is manipulated for larger ends
> and for the greater good as determined by scientific aristocracy. It is
> assumed, then, that the scientist-shamans know best what course
> humankind should take ... While surprises may appear in these sto-
> ries (e.g. the Mule mutant), it is assumed that no surprise will be too
> great or too unexpected to overcome the firm grasp of science upon
> human destiny. This is essentially the assumption that science can
> produce a surprise-free future for humankind.
>
> (Herbert, quoted in O'Reilly 1981: 87)

At the same time, it is worth stressing, lest my account here should seem too harsh, the excitement with which many readers respond to the power of Asimov's imaginative conception. Even critics with negative comments on the books concede their effectiveness; Manlove, for instance, calls it 'this brilliant work'. That has a great deal to do with the scale and range of Asimov's imagination; to produce a novel of ideas, a novel that philosophically engages with questions of historiography (which is to say, the nature and theory of history, the way history works) and epistemology (questions of knowledge and the ways in which it is possible to know anything), and that does so on the largest possible scales of space and time, really does sweep the reader along. And in the sense that this novel approaches the sort of sublimity associated with vastness, Asimov is working the same aesthetic line as E. E. 'Doc' Smith. He stages his psychohistory via a series of dramatically effective unveilings of deeper truths, more hidden mysteries. The Foundation organisation itself is hidden behind the façade of a group compiling the *Encyclopedia Galactica*, and only reveals itself during the course of the first novel. With the reversals of the Mule, Asimov pulls away another curtain to reveal the Second Foundation. By the time we have moved through several books in the sequence, to *Foundation's Edge* (1982), Asimov has revealed an even deeper truth: that the universe itself in its present form owes its existence to an ancient race of Eternals who chose from a plethora of possibilities the universe we now inhabit, in which man is the only sentient life form. A greater plan, similarly deterministic, underlies his character Seldon's conception of history as something to be controlled.

This aesthetic of scale is more sophisticated in its workings-out than in the Pulp writing of the 1920s and 1930s, but it relates symbolically to the same ideological concerns. As John Huntington argues:

> At the core of much SF fantasy is an identification with power. We see it in recent SF by an exaltation in sheer size: empires war with ships the size of planets. A student once explained to me that SF was interesting and important because the weapons it imagined were capable of destroying a planet, even a universe. How trivial the cowboy's six-shooter was by comparison. Such an observation is not entirely naïve.
>
> (Huntington 1989: 44)

SF IN THE 1960S AND 1970S

If 'Golden Age' SF mirrors the bullishness of the American experience of the 1940s, there are many examples of 1950s SF that mirror an increasing unease. From Asimov's confidence that science, applied properly, could solve all problems, we find in the 1950s an increasing scepticism. At the beginning of the 1950s American society was convulsed with a paranoid campaign against communism led by Senator Joe McCarthy: people were publicly condemned for not embracing 'American values' with enough zeal. McCarthy believed that agents from the Soviet Union were infiltrating American society and turning, as he saw it, 'good' American citizens into secret 'evil' communists. This climate of political paranoia, with its fearful conformity and obsessive focusing on the Alien as Enemy, fed directly through into SF imaginations. Jack Finney wrote a novel called *Body Snatchers* in 1955, in which a small American town is invaded by alien spores from space that grow into exact copies of individual human beings whilst destroying their originals. This was made into a highly regarded film in 1956, *Invasion of the Body Snatchers*, directed by Don Siegel. The effectiveness of both texts depends to a large extent on how finely balanced they are as political satire. Indeed, they can be read *both* as McCartheyite scaremongering – communists from an alien place are infiltrating our American towns and wiping out their American values, and the worst of it is they look *exactly like Americans* – and as left-wing liberal satire on the ideological climate of conformism that McCarthyism produced, where the lack of emotion of the pod-people corresponds to the ethical blind eyes turned by Americans to the persecutions of their fellows by over-zealous McCarthyites.

Critics are divided as to exactly when SF stopped being a minority interest and became a mass phenomenon. According to Edward James, it was during the 1950s that SF experienced a 'boom in America' which led to an explosive 'growth in SF readership'. James thinks that this readership was 'inspired perhaps by worries about the future (for the cold war fostered paranoia of all kinds)' (James 1994: 84). According to John Huntington, on the other hand, it was not until the 1960s and what is called 'New Wave SF' that the genre became a genuinely mass, popular phenomenon. It is certainly the case that during the 1960s a number of 'cult' novels achieved enormous international popularity, starting with devoted fans on university campuses and spreading out.

Three such texts are Tolkien's *The Lord of the Rings* (1954–55); as Fantasy, this work is outside the range of a study of SF), Heinlein's massive *Stranger in a Strange Land* (1961) and Herbert's *Dune* (1965). According to Huntington (1989: vii), 'by the sixties SF had crossed a boundary and ceased to be the literature of only an intensely devoted minority'. The broad popularity in the late 1960s of *Stranger in a Strange Land* and *Dune* is a phenomenon quite unlike the comparatively select popularity of 'Golden Age SF'. Huntington explicitly links this burgeoning popularity with the shifting ideological tenor of the times:

> The growth of new wave SF in the sixties can be seen as a rendering of attitudes implicit in the SF of the middle and late fifties. It is not accidental that the flourishing of the new wave in SF coincides with a decade of political activism and of skepticism about technological solutions to social and environmental problems.
>
> (Huntington 1989: 2)

There was also a shift in the economic dynamics of publishing during the 1950s and 1960s. Where magazine publishing had been the norm throughout the 1940s, in the 1950s the balance shifted towards books. Publishers woke up particularly to the possibilities of paperback production, and by the 1960s magazines were experiencing a gradual decline in circulation numbers, whilst more and more novels were being published. A number of writers began working out their ideas at novel length, rather than 'fixing up' novels from previously published shorter pieces. And much of the (arguably) ideologically monolithic writing of the Golden Age became subject to critique; its underlying assumptions about culture and society were challenged. In place of a rationalist belief in the effectiveness of technology and machinery to solve all human problems, there came an avant-garde 'experimental literature' fascination with the artistic possibilities of those very problems, and in particular a paranoid aesthetic in which all large systems were seen as the enemies of individual difference.

NEW WAVE

In part this is encompassed by the phrase Huntington makes reference to: 'New Wave SF'. The term 'New Wave' describes a loose grouping of writers from the 1960s and 1970s who, in reaction to the established conventions of SF, produced avant-garde, radical or fractured science fictions. All the labels concocted for literary movements are problematic, but the label 'New Wave' is more problematic than most. As Damien Broderick notes, this 'reaction against genre exhaustion' was 'never quite formalised and often repudiated by its major exemplars' (in James and Mendlesohn 2003: 49). The term was initially associated with the London magazine *New Worlds*, which became a venue for experimental and envelope-pushing fiction under the editorship of Michael Moorcock from 1964–1971. Moorcock himself identified various writers as promising templates of a new style of passionate, ironic and original sort of SF, amongst them J. G. Ballard, Brian Aldiss and John Brunner.

The London bias of the movement was leavened by a number of prominent American writers, Thomas M. Disch, John Sladek and Samuel R. Delany (although Delany, seen as New Wave by many, has repudiated the label), who all came to live in the UK at this time. But critics are again divided as to how far New Wave aesthetics penetrated American SF; a chapter title in Roger Luckhurst's recent cultural history of SF asks: 'was there an American New Wave?' (Luckhurst 2005: 160). In *New Worlds* Ballard called for a comprehensive rejection of SF cliché:

> Science fiction should turn its back on space, on interstellar travel, extra-terrestrial life forms, galactic wars and the overlap of these ideas that spreads across the margins of nine-tenths of magazine s-f. Great writer though he was, I'm convinced H. G. Wells has had a disastrous influence on the subsequent course of science fiction ... similarly, I think, science fiction must jettison its present narrative forms and plots.
>
> (quoted in James 1994: 169–70)

'New Wave' is usually taken to be an attempt to raise the literary quality of SF, which to a certain extent it was; but what Ballard's remarks make plain is the extent to which it was also a reaction to the sedimentary weight of the genre's backlist, which new writers were beginning to feel as oppressive. By the 1960s the SF 'megatext' was so large that bringing novelty to the SF novel was becoming harder. What the New

Wave did was to take a genre that had been, in its popular mode, more concerned with content and 'ideas' than form, style or aesthetics and pay much greater attention to the latter three terms.

For many fans this amounted to a betrayal of what SF was all about. In typically grumpy form, author and SF fan Kingsley Amis declared 'the effects of the New Wave' to have been 'uniformly deleterious'.

> The new mode abandoned the hallmarks of traditional science fiction; its emphasis on content rather than style and treatment, its avoid-ance of untethered fantasy and its commitment instead to logic, motive and common sense ... [instead] in came shock tactics, tricks with typography, one-line chapters, strained metaphors, obscurities, obscenities, drugs, Oriental religions and left-wing politics.
>
> (Amis 1981: 22)

This is a deliberate travesty of the movement, and the self-satisfaction with which Amis announced that 'by 1974 or so the New Wave was being declared officially over' was deluded and wrong-headed. For fans of Amis's persuasion it would be truer to say that the Golden Age never went away. SF continued to be written according to the protocols against which the New Wave was reacting: Murray Leinster, Gordon Dickson, Fred Saberhagen, Ben Bova, H. Beam Piper and various others produced a great quantity of hard-edged, technologically oriented and often militaristic SF. Their spiritual home was Campbell's *Analog* (the name for *Astounding* after 1960), and this sort of writing had an enthusiastic following throughout the period.

In fact, the major achievements of 1960s and 1970s SF worked dialectically between 'New Wave' ideas and Golden Age groundings. The scale and ambition of *Dune* have been discussed in Chapter 1; it is a novel that owes much to the effects of scale found in Pulp and Golden Age SF, although Herbert deploys them for different reasons. In part, this is because the mystical agenda of the novel, combined with its abandonment of technological nova, marks *Dune* very much as a product of the countercultural environment of the 1960s, something enhanced by the ubiquity of the drug 'Spice' in Herbert's imagined world. A work like Heinlein's *Stranger in a Strange Land* seems today even more obviously rooted in the 'drop-out' hippy counterculture of its time. Some critics have expressed surprise that a book by so right-wing, libertarian and gun-obsessed a writer as Heinlein should have achieved cult status amongst university students and hippies. But *Stranger in a Strange Land* lengthily and deliberately adopts the perspective of difference that identified it easily with the countercultural beliefs of many of its readers. Its central character, Valentine Michael Smith, has an outsider's perspective on Earth, being born on Mars and raised by Martians. His adventures on our planet allow him to act as spokesman for a number of anti-status quo positions; his own philosophy is founded on the idea of 'grokking', a word Heinlein coined that has now become part of the English language (to 'grok' means to establish a rapport with, to empathise with someone intuitively, something the telepathic Smith can manage easily). In the novel this becomes the foundation for a defence of free love. 'Sex', says one of the characters, elaborating the Michael Smith gospel, '*should* be a means of happiness.'

> The code says 'thou shalt not covet thy neighbour's wife.' The result? Reluctant chastity, adultery, jealousy, bitterness, blows and sometimes murder, broken homes and twisted children – and furtive little passes degrading to woman and man. Is this commandment ever obeyed? ... Now comes [Valentine Michael Smith] and says: 'there is no need to covet my wife ... love her! There's no limit to her love, we have everything to gain – and nothing to lose but fear and guilt and hatred and jealousy.' This proposition is incredible.
>
> (Heinlein, *Stranger in a Strange Land* (1961): 366)

For a culture fascinated with difference and diversity, Smith becomes an iconic Messiah figure. The blend of hedonism and mysticism represented in the book captures exactly the way the science-fictional point of difference can become the platform for a cultural movement that specifically defines itself as different from mainstream culture. At the same time, as Aldiss points out, Heinlein's book is also the straightforward inheritor of a 'well established and respectable pulp tradition of the all-powerful male, so largely epitomised in John W. Campbell's swaggering intergalactic heroes' (Aldiss 1973: 274).

At the close of this brief survey chapter, there are two further things worth stressing about SF from the 1960s to the present day. One is that the challenges to the totalising assumptions of 'Golden Age' SF manifested themselves in more fundamental ways than just the subject matter of the texts themselves. Every single twentieth-century author I have mentioned in this chapter so far has been white and male. One of the most significant aspects of the development of the genre has been the growth of authors of colour; another is the rise of women authors of SF, so much so that it is probably fair to say that the present-day giants of the field are Ursula Le Guin and Octavia Butler. But even more significant than this eruption of alterity into the structures of production of SF itself is the enormous growth in popularity of the genre. Partly this has been novel-led, with certain authors and certain texts (I have already mentioned Heinlein and Herbert) achieving first cult and then international success. But a more significant factor, in terms of the sheer numbers of people attracted to SF, has been TV and cinema. First came the success of *Star Trek*, which was, in truth, slightly belated. Paramount made three series of the show (1966–9) and then cancelled it, following only modest ratings; but a dedicated fan base and a growing audience created by re-runs through the 1970s eventually turned *Trek* into the most successful televisual SF phenomenon. By the mid-1970s the climate was right for a single cinema film, *Star Wars* (1977), to ignite an astonishing popular engagement with SF. It is due to *Star Wars* that the cinematic climate of Hollywood shifted so thoroughly towards SF, and that as a result almost all the twenty top-grossing films of all time are science-fictional (the *Star Wars* films, *ET*, *Jurassic Park*, the *Terminator* films, the *Alien* sequence and *Independence Day* have each made many hundreds of millions and even billions of dollars).

A more detailed examination of post-1960s SF takes place in the next three chapters, which look at the rise of women's SF and at questions of race and of technology in the genre. But I want to finish this chapter by looking at a text that exhibits this recursive tendency of SF, which is to say the way in which SF texts today make use of and refer back to the very history of the genre I have been sketching in this chapter. A film such as *Star Wars* exists in very close relationship with the conventions and strengths of Pulp and Golden Age SF.

CASE STUDY: *STAR WARS* (1977) AND INTERTEXTUALITY

It was *Star Wars* that jump-started SF in the 1970s, turning it from a vigorous but fairly small-scale genre into the dominant mode of cinematic discourse. It is a crucial text for any study of post war SF, not only because of its astonishing success and the vitality of the fan culture which has grown up around it, but because it marks a sort of way-station in the literary traditions of the genre. *Star Wars* mediates the Pulp SF heritage of the Golden Age and translates it into something larger-scale, bigger-budget, more sophisticated and glossy.

One of the joys of *Star Wars* is precisely the way it straddles the traditions of SF, the homely virtues of melodrama and adventure that we associate with Pulp SF, on the one hand, and the techno-sophisticated brilliance of 1980s special-effects SF on the other. It looks back and it looks forward. In fact, it is the backward-looking aspects of the film that are dominant. So it is no coincidence that this film begins with the legend 'A Long Time Ago, in a Galaxy Far Away … '. It is not just the styling of this film that looks backwards rather than forwards, so too do the underlying values and ideology. What I mean by this is that, in obvious ways, the supposedly far-future technology of *Star Wars* is actually old fashioned, 1940s technology. For instance, the X-Wing fighters are Second World War fighters and bombers. Scenes such as the one in which Luke and Obi-Wan go into the Mos Eisley bar are based on the ubiquitous bar-room scene of western movies. The reason for this, I think, is that it is precisely this bygone age of heroism that appeals to George Lucas, the director, and therefore to us, his audience. But this appeals to Lucas for a particular reason: the political ideology underlying these films is profoundly conservative.

However, it needs to be stressed that *Star Wars* laid the future foundations for SF in the 1980s and 1990s. Of course, the first reaction of the crowds queuing to see it in long lines outside cinemas in 1977 was not how old fashioned it was, but how futuristic, how advanced and prophetic it looked. This is the way ideology masks itself: it pretends to be forward-looking to disguise its conservatism. But there is something more here, a sense in which this is the creative tension at the core of the *Star Wars* films, the contradiction that powers their unique appeal. The paradox is embodied by the second trilogy of films made by Lucas between 1999 and 2005 (*The Phantom Menace, Attack of the Clones* and *Revenge of the Sith*). Because the three new films are prequels, they are necessarily set back in the history of the *Star Wars* universe, and accordingly their styling and design must embody that history, must in some sense suggest 'old-fashionedness' when compared to the styling and design of the original movies. But because these films are actually being made twenty years *after* the original films – twenty years in which film technology and especially the technology of special effects have matured enormously – they are also, necessarily, going to look *more modern*, more up to date, more futuristic. Cinemagoers would be loath to pay to see a film that demonstrated 1950s-level special effects, although that would be one way of effectively retro-styling the movie. So the new *Star Wars* prequels embody a curious relation to history. They are simultaneously newer and older, more futuristic and more solidly set in the past. This curious circumstance neatly encapsulates the way any given SF text is positioned in relation to history and the future.

In a sense it is the contradictions of these films that give them so powerful and complex an appeal. There is, we can see, an unresolved tension between future-vision and past-vision that runs right through the original trilogy, and that manifests itself in, for instance, the way the films demonise technology. Technology is associated with the bad guys, the Empire: the Imperial stormtroopers are kitted up to look like robots; their all-machine worlds are entirely devoid of vegetation or any other organic, 'natural' landscaping; their enormous spaceships harness technology to immensely destructive ends. The rebels, on the other hand, are associated with forests and green colours, and most obviously with the organic 'Force' that supersedes the power of machines. But these are films that simultaneously relish and delight in their technology, the spectacle of their special effects, the delight of the spaceships and robots and all the *stuff*. As Scott Bukatman puts it, the film evidences a 'struggle between antitechnological narrative and hyper-technological aesthetic' (Bukatman 1993: 347). What is interesting in this struggle is the way both the ubiquity of the technology and the universal immanence of the 'Force' enact a web of intertextual quotations and allusions that binds the whole text together. That is what these nova symbolise: the linkage and coherence of intertextuality itself, the web of quotation and allusion in which all texts are located.

It is hard to deny, certainly, that watching a film like *Star Wars* as an SF fan is a process of identifying a web of allusions and quotations from SF texts, particularly Golden Age texts. Lucas's first ambition was to make a modern version of the 1930s comic-strip and matinée film series *Flash Gordon*. He researched this idea but abandoned it because the estate that owned the *Flash Gordon* copyright wanted too much money. So Lucas invented his own imaginary universe, one that owes something to the mood and tone of *Flash Gordon* but which loses the elements of high-camp fun that characterised the original. The feel of the *Star Wars* universe owes more to such Space Opera classic authors as Edgar Rice Burroughs and, especially, E. E. 'Doc' Smith, whose *Lensman* novels are evidently a direct source. Most obviously Smithian is the scale of Lucas's universe and the artefacts in it, in particular the Death Star, an entire artificial planet that destroys other planets. Smith wrote of an entire planet aimed and fired at Earth at faster-than-light speeds, like a vast cannonball. Lucas may also have been thinking of the AKKA, a super-weapon from Jack Williamson's *The Legion of Space* (1934), which exterminates whole fleets of spaceships at the push of a button.

Lucas also deliberately modelled his screenplay on a classic of Japanese cinema, Akira Kurosawa's *The Hidden Fortress* (1958), in which a princess and her loyal general undertake a perilous quest to recover their rightful treasure, aided only by two bumbling and comical servants. Lucas has consistently expressed his admiration for Kurosawa as a film-maker, and in *Star Wars* he not only borrows specific elements of this film's narrative, most particularly the two servants who become the droids R2D2 and C3PO, but also goes some way towards aping Kurosawa's characteristic epic-sweep directing style. Critics have spent some time on this high-culture source for *Star Wars*, but even this act of homage is part of a popular-culture Pulp tradition: another Kurosawa film, *The Seven Samurai* (1954), was remade as the incomparable western *The Magnificent Seven* (1960). Of course, there is the element of the western in *Star Wars* too, and this helps give it its distinctively American tone. But surely more significant for the film is its heritage in films of the Second World War, most notably *The Dam Busters* (1954) and *633 Squadron* (1964), from which the film's ending is taken. It is the Second World War, and specifically its ethical contrast between the ideologies of the Allies and the Nazis, that gives *Star*

Wars its moral framework. In particular, Peter Cushing's character Grand Moff Tarkin, with his Nazi-style uniform and his merciless style so evocative of war-film Nazi villains, helps link the Empire with that particular 1940s manifestation of evil.

Lucas also fills his film with explicit references to the traditions of American SF. The scenes shot on Tatooine, Luke Skywalker's home-world, make very obvious reference to *Dune*. In fact, this (relatively brief) cinematic representation of a desert world is rather more powerful than David Lynch's feeble film of *Dune* (1984) itself. Also derived from Herbert's *Dune*, I think, is the blend of the East – in the guises of the patronising Bedouin variants, the Jawas, as well as the whole bag-and-baggage of 'the Force', which seems to me a translation into populist terms of Herbert's more arcane mysticism – and the West. Tatooine is the location for the frontiersmen and outlaws, like the wild west. Luke's father is a sodbuster, and the bar in Mos Eisley and Han Solo himself represent the gunslinger side of George Stevens' 1953 film *Shane*. Peter Nicholls thinks that Lucas's 'decadent Galactic Empire' was 'perhaps inspired by Isaac Asimov's *Foundation* series' (Nicholls 1981: 571). The Kurosawa-based robots certainly do owe a lot to Asimov, the formulator (with John Campbell) of the once-famous 'three laws of robotics', which these robots seem to follow, and the writer of a great many novels and stories in which the 'humanity' of robots becomes a key feature. The alien 'Ewoks' in *Return of the Jedi*, little furry teddy-bear creatures who, with enormous implausibility, defeat the heavily armed and armoured shock troops of the Empire using clubs and stones in the trilogy's final battle, bear so close a resemblance to H. Beam Piper's 'Fuzzies', from a series of novels that began in 1962 with *Little Fuzzy*, that Piper's estate considered suing for breach of copyright.

SF intertextuality, then, is one of the key ways in which this film text operates, and our response to the film is conditioned by that fact. The intriguingly double-edged relationship of the film to its own imag-ined history, and to the history of the genre of which it is some sort of apotheosis, exemplifies the concerns of that history. To put this another way, one of the factors of SF fandom is an intimate knowledge of the canon and conventions of SF itself; in short, a knowledge of the history of the evolution of the form itself. This gives the initiate a double read-ing or viewing experience: the text, such as *Star Wars*, can be enjoyed on its own terms and simultaneously as a matrix of quotation, allusion, pastiche and reference. Many texts outside SF can be enjoyed in this latter manner, too, of course; but it is the intensity of the devotion of SF fans to their subject that permits this dense network of intertexts (texts that connect with many other texts) in a popular idiom. The SF text is both about its professed subject and also, always, about SF. This is where the points made in the first chapter come together. *Star Wars* is both forward looking, which is to say futuristic, and backward looking, or nostalgic, but SF's backward orientation means more than the fact that it is set 'a long time ago, in a galaxy far away'. *Star Wars* looks backwards over the history of the genre itself, in that it incorporates Smith, Asimov, Herbert, *Flash Gordon* and more. It juxtaposes past and future so thoroughly, in so immanent a manner, that it inhabits the contradiction that is at the heart of any 'history of the future'. When this text makes reference to its all-powerful 'Force' that binds and connects everything, that controls the agents' actions but can also be controlled by them, that permits tremendous feats within the SF idiom, what it is really doing is invoking the imaginative potency of the genre within which it exists, the intertextual power of the science-fictional mode itself. This amounts to a definition of what the Force is: it is SF, linking and empowering the individual text across the network of SF history.

3

SF AND GENDER

One of the major theoretical projects of the second wave of feminism is the investigation of gender and sexuality as social constructs ... The stock conventions of science fiction – time travel, alternate worlds, entropy, relativism, the search for a unified field theory – can be used metaphorically and metonymically as powerful ways of exploring the construction of 'woman'.

(Sarah Lefanu 1988: 4–5)

FEMINIST SCIENCE FICTION

One of the most notable features of contemporary SF is how high a proportion of the best writers working in the field use the idiom to interrogate the logic of 'gender'. This chapter looks to explore various aspects of the way SF's emphasis on gender shifted from being defined by unspoken masculinist assumptions of 'the proper role for women' to the more sophisticated approaches to questions of gender associated with the first and second waves of feminist theory from the 1960s to the present day. It will close with a reading of Ursula Le Guin's 1969 novel *The Left Hand of Darkness*. But it is worth noting at the beginning how contentious Le Guin's position is within the body of female SF, as a means of pointing up that 'female SF' is not a straightforwardly or narrowly single quantity. *The Left Hand of Darkness* is one of the acknowledged classics of SF; it won, for instance, both a Hugo and a Nebula award, two of the most prestigious awards in SF publishing. But much of the feminist criticism of Le Guin is rather cold, sometimes dismissive and occasionally outright hostile. Critic Sarah Lefanu finds Le Guin's writing fatally limited, too character-based to be SF at all, and not very well realised as character studies either. Of the characters in *The Left Hand of Darkness* Lefanu asks: 'how realistic are [they]? Who remembers what they look like? Or what they say? Or feel?' (Lefanu 1988: 143). Lefanu prefers SF writer Joanna Russ. Joanna Russ herself thought *The Left Hand of Darkness* a failure, though an honourable one. Jenny Wolmark's *Aliens and Others: Science Fiction, Feminism and Postmodernism* (1994) omits Le Guin altogether, and the critic Susan Bassnett, whilst conceding that Le Guin has been 'extremely popular and successful' for 'both adults and children', none the less points out in Lucie Armitt's edited collection *Where No Man Has Gone Before* (1991) that she 'has not always been treated very kindly by those critics who have actually considered her work' (Armitt 1991: 50). There is a great deal of valuable criticism of SF from a feminist or women's writing point of view. In order to understand why as talented a writer as Le Guin has received such a poor showing in that criticism, and why her novels are so consistently judged in terms of her representation of gender, we need briefly to put her work into context.

One of the reasons why feminist criticism of SF has a radicalism that seems almost old fashioned when compared with the subtler, more complex feminisms that characterise criticism as a whole is that women are a relatively recent arrival in the realm of SF writing itself. 'Golden Age' SF, the argument goes, was almost exclusively male; it was written by men, purchased by men or boys; its conventions were shaped by the passions and interests of adolescent males, that is to say its focus was on technology as embodied particularly by big, gleaming machines with lots of moving parts, physical prowess, war, two-dimensional male heroes, adventure and excitement. From the dawn of SF (whenever we choose to date that) through to the end of the 1950s the female audience for SF was small, and those women who were interested in reading it did so with a sense of themselves as alienated or at least sidelined spectators.

This is too crude and reductive an account of the matter, however. As Roger Luckhurst points out, although 'SF is often stereotyped for embody-

ing a particular form of male immaturity', in fact 'this is, like all stereotypes, ill-informed'. SF throughout its history has been fascinated by
gender identities and relations, and many examples can be adduced of
SF texts that dramatise, for instance, threats posed to ordinary life by
rampant women or feminised aliens. 'What the feminist intervention of
the 1970s did effect, though,' Luckhurst points out, 'was a new reflexiv-
ity about the conventions of SF, exposing how a genre that praised itself
for its limitless imagination and its power to refuse norms had largely
reproduced "patriarchal attitudes" without questioning them for much
of its existence' (Luckhurst 2005: 181–2). Moreover, in the words of
Sarah LeFanu, although 'science fiction is popularly conceived as male
territory, boys' own adventure stories with little to interest a female
readership', in fact this description only applies to 'the heyday of magazine science fiction, the 1930s and 1940s, but even then there were
women writers, like C. L. Moore and Leigh Brackett' (Lefanu 1988: 2).
The difference, she points out, is that such women more often than not
'assumed a male voice and non-gender-specific names to avoid prejudice
on the part of editors and readers alike'. Women who wished to become
involved, as writers or readers, had to assume a certain masculine identity, to become what we might call (after Russ's novel) Female Men. The
Tiptree experiment (see below) in a sense focused exactly these prejudices, but at a more gender-aware time.

The point about this 'feminist intervention' was that it was constituted by more than just academic critics or feminist theorists. Two
things in particular need to be kept in mind. The first was the establish-
ment, slowly at first but then, as it gained in popularity and sales, more
rapidly, of a body of SF novels written by women and read in large part
by women. This is something that happened particularly in the 1960s
and 1970s, and there are three names associated with the success of this
new mode. They are: Marion Zimmer Bradley, Andre Norton and
Ursula Le Guin. Bradley has written dozens of novels set on a planet
called Darkover, the chronicles of which span the world's history from a
pre-technological, medievalised culture to a spacefaring technological
one. Andre Norton's series of Fantasy novels set on what she calls the
Witch World provided the first, and one of the most popular, rework-
ings of the Tolkien style of Fantasy Epic from a female point of view.
Ursula Le Guin's 'Hainish' cycle includes some of the most acclaimed

works in SF, amongst them *The Left Hand of Darkness* and *The Dispossessed* (1974).

Marion Zimmer Bradley began by writing male-centred, technological SF derived heavily from the Golden Age conventions; but as her confidence, and audience, grew, she shifted her perspective to female-centred studies that explored concerns more crucial to her own life. One of her earliest Darkover books, *Star of Danger* (1965), has a 'Boy's Own' plot about two young lads travelling through a wilderness area of the planet and undergoing a series of adventures whilst on the run from a bandit chief. There are no major female characters in this novel and virtually no women of any sort. More than this, the protagonist, Larry Montry from Earth, falls under the spell of the unreconstructed machismo of Darkover culture. He meets a young nobleman of that world, Kennard Dalton, after bravely fighting off a gang of toughs. Triumphing in this fight wins Larry respect. Darkovans, or at any rate male Darkovans, find it incomprehensible that people on Earth rely on the police to sort out their difficulties; on Darkover if an individual is wronged, it is that individual's duty to obtain retribution. Earth's is 'a government of laws', but, says Kennard proudly, 'ours is a government of men, because laws can't be anything but the expression of men who make them' (Bradley 1965: 82). At no point in the novel are the masculinist prejudices of the Darkovian world challenged, or even mentioned without a sort of starry-eyed respect. But a later Darkover novel, *Stormqueen* (1978), is more women-oriented and marks the feminist evolution of its author's sensibilities. It is set several hundred years before the Darkover of *Star of Danger*, in an age before the technologies of space flight have reached the planet, and it is far more explicit about the perils so macho a society involves for the women who live in it. One character, about to make a sort of marriage of convenience to a powerful noble, explains to her son that 'life is not easy for a woman unprotected'. The alternative to this unwanted marriage would be an effective concubinage: 'for me there would be nothing but to be a drudge or a sewing woman' (Bradley 1978: 6). As the novel progresses, the main character reveals telepathic capacities, known as *laran*, and the book explores the compensations that *laran* offers to women in a brutal and oppressive society. Bradley has talked about her shift of interests. In the introduction to *The Best of Marion Zimmer Bradley*, a collection of her short fiction published in 1985, she said her 'current enthusiasms ... are Gay Rights and Women's Rights – I think Women's Liberation is the great event of the twentieth century, not Space Exploration. One is a great change in human consciousness; the latter is only predictable technology, and I am bored by technology' (Bradley 1985: 13).

This emphasis on the affective, the personal, rather than the technological was also the reason for the second significant catalyst from the 1960s, one that introduced a large body of female fans to SF, fans that had previously been put off by the Golden Age genre widely perceived (with only partial justice) as a series of masculinist 'boys and their toys' posturings. This catalyst was the TV series *Star Trek*. Indeed, although its importance is often underplayed, it seems clear to me that *Star Trek* brought more women to SF than all the other authors mentioned so far put together. It remains a cornerstone of female SF fandom. The success of this syndicated show in the late 1960s, particularly amongst a female audience, brought hundreds of thousands of women to the genre. And this was a success based less on the technological or male-ego strands of the show and more on the way *Star Trek* represented, in the first instance, human interaction and the social dynamic as being at the heart of the SF story and, in the second instance, and less obviously, because *Trek*, unusually for a 1960s US TV show, was interested in representing difference. The encounter with the alien is at the core of *Star Trek* and of most SF; and questions of difference, of alien-ness and otherness, were also powerful and relevant to the female perspective on the old patriarchal world. This is why the show built up, and maintains, so large a female audience. Nor is this female audience merely a body of passive viewers; there is a vigorous and wide-ranging body of fanzines and even fan-authored novels based upon the *Star Trek* universe. As Henry Jenkins has exhaustively demonstrated, '*Star Trek* fandom is a predominantly female response to mass media texts, with the majority of fanzines edited by and written by women for a largely female readership' (Tulloch and Jenkins 1995: 196–7).

It was this issue of difference, where 'alien' becomes an encoding of 'woman', that featured prominently in the work of the 1970s new wave of radical female SF writers. This was a much more populated era of women's SF in terms of the number of women writing SF. But there are three names that crop up again and again in the criticism, so I mention them here: Octavia Butler, Marge Piercy and Joanna Russ. Russ is perhaps the most often cited. Her most famous novel, *The Female Man* (1975), presents a four-fold perspective of women's experience of the world, including a women-only utopian realm called Whileaway. Russ is one of the most committed feminist writers and critics, and *The Female Man* has received a great deal of respectful criticism. But Gwyneth Jones is surely right when she judges this novel a relative failure compared with some others of Russ's fictions. It is set partly on the planet Whileaway, where there are no men, only women, and the utopian possibilities of this world are contrasted with the trajectories of female existence on other possible worlds where women are oppressed to one degree or another. Russ has written about all-female societies elsewhere, most notably in the story 'When It Changed' (1972), but, as Jones points out, the female society in that story is 'not unreasonably idealised'. The women have the faults and strengths of 'the whole of humanity'. By the time of *The Female Man* the all-woman world 'has been got at. Its inhabitants have become female characters in a feminist science fiction, their vices and virtues bowdlerised and engineered precisely to fit the current demands of sexual politics.' Russ's novel is effectively hijacked by a feminist agenda: '*When It Changed* is feminist fiction, *The Female Man* is feminist satire' (Jones 1999: 125–6).

This thought-experiment of a female-only society remains a staple of contemporary SF. To mention only two of the many recent treatments of it: in the near-future world of Tricia Sullivan's *Maul* (2003) almost all men have been wiped out by a Y-chromosome-specific plague. Liz William's *Banner of Souls* (2005) is set in a much more distant future in which, for the Matriarchy of Mars, men are nothing more than a distant historical memory. Both novels do interesting things with their premises of a female-dominated society; for neither writer is this a necessarily utopian development.

Of the other names mentioned, Octavia Butler, as a writer both female and black, has an especially acute perspective on issues of 'alien as other'. Her *Xenogenesis* series is examined in Chapter 4 of the present study. Marge Piercy's feminist utopia *Woman on the Edge of Time* (1976) is often contrasted with *The Left Hand of Darkness* as a 'successful' version of a world without gender. Another name worth introducing at this point, although not one that seems immediately appropriate in a discussion of SF written by women, is James Tiptree Jr.

Tiptree was the pseudonym of Alice Sheldon, a writer of enormous gifts. Oddly, those gifts, whilst rarely doubted, may have less currency amongst fans nowadays than one feature of her life story. As many female writers had done before her, she chose a male pseudonym to publish under (the surname came from a brand of marmalade), and she responded to enquiries from editors and fans with many biographical details – such as the time she had spent working in the Pentagon and her role in setting up the CIA – except her gender. Accordingly she was assumed by many in the SF world to be male. The general revelation in the late 1970s that she was in fact a woman embarrassed many, and two notable figures in SF in particular: Robert Silverberg, who had written an introduction to Tiptree's collection *Warm Worlds and Otherwise* (1975) rubbishing the suggestion that she could possibly be a woman, and Ursula Le Guin (b. 1929), who had prevented Tiptree from adding a signature to a feminist petition on the grounds that she was male. Sarah Lefanu quotes Silverberg's dotty certainty: 'it has been suggested that Tiptree is female, a theory that I find absurd, for there is to me something ineluctably masculine about Tiptree's writing … lean, muscular, supple, Hemmingwayesque', and then quotes his more elegant retraction ('she fooled me beautifully, along with everyone else, and called into question the entire notion of what is "masculine" or "feminine" in fiction'). But as Lefanu herself points out, 'there is something dangerous about seeing masculinity and femininity in such essentialist terms' (Lefanu 1988: 122–3)

It is certainly true that some of Tiptree's stories do make penetrating points about gender, most famously 'The Women Men Don't See' (1973) in which a group of women are as happy to live in 'the chinks of the world machine' of an alien spacecraft as in the interstices of a male-dominated society. In 'The Screwfly Solution' (1977) the widespread murders of women turn into a global holocaust, as an alien agent, looking to depopulate the globe prior to moving in, causes men to confuse sexual lust and blood lust. It is a genuinely chilling and upsetting tale that works both as a caricature of conventional male attitudes and as a properly SF intervention into a plausibly extrapolated world.

But her stories range far beyond gender issues. 'I'll be waiting for you when the swimming pool is empty' (1971) is a rather crude satire on the 1960s Peace Corps, in which infectious 'American' values overwhelm the native cultures with which it has contact – although the story's energetic comedy saves it from being po-faced.

'The Girl Who Was Plugged In' (1974) nicely satirises corporate commodification and reification. Both 'Faithful to thee, Terra, in our fashion' (1968) and 'And I awoke and found me here on the cold hill's side' (1971) are clever explorations of colonial and post-colonial logics, from both sides of the equation. Acknowledging that 'James Tiptree' was in fact Alice Sheldon should not mean that we can only read her penetrating, chilling and brilliant stories as limited to the problematic of being a woman.

Having said that, it would be distorting to deny that many of the generation of female writers of the 1960s and 1970s did deliberately focus gender concerns through the lens of SF. An essay by Joanna Russ that was first published in the SF magazine *Vertex* in 1971 is often cited by feminist critics of SF as a classic articulation of these issues. In that essay, Russ declared that 'one would think science fiction the perfect literary mode in which to explore (and explode) our assumptions about "innate" values and "natural" social arrangements'. But whilst 'some of this has been done', Russ points out that 'speculation about the innate personality differences between men and women, about family structure, about sex, in short about gender roles, does not exist at all'. The essay is called 'The Image of Women in Science Fiction'. Russ says she chose that title rather than 'Women in Science Fiction' because 'if I had chosen the latter, there would have been very little to say. There are plenty of images of women in science fiction. There are hardly any women' (Russ 1972: 79–80). Even today there is still a sense in which the SF contact with the alien remains a powerful medium for expressing female perspectives.

WOMEN AND ALIENS

The point here, as throughout this study, is not that SF articulates the difference of women in the sense that women 'are different' from men. There is SF that basically says just that, but it is not SF properly located in the discourse of difference; instead it is simply a means of reinstating the 'normality' of the male experience and the 'deviance from the norm' that is women, and it therefore remains a sexist discourse. A genuine discourse of alterity would examine the ways gender constructs differ-ence, the way a person's gender is conceived in terms of difference. It might use an expression of material difference, which is to say non-humanity – a space alien, a machine, a symbolic novum – as a means of exploring what it is like to have the label 'different' imposed on a per-son by some normalising system.

These are some of the ways 'the alien' can be used to encode the female experience. Marleen Barr has talked about the way 'the female' in patriarchal society is already constituted as alien: women are 'alien in our culture which insists that "to be human is to be male" ' (Barr 1987: 31). Robin Roberts, in her book *A New Species* (1993), has looked in detail at the way 'the alien' has been used to figure female experience. Jenny Wolmark has also worked through this theme, bringing in some of the insights of postmodern theory. Wolmark finds merit in those books that challenge the more reactionary SF notion of 'alien' as villain, the sort of representation to be found in texts such as Robert Heinlein's *Starship Troopers* (1959), in which a quasi-fascist military society is engaged in a prolonged and bloody interstellar war against repulsive giant insectoid aliens. Heinlein's giant bugs are one apotheosis of 'the enemy'; they have none of the qualities humanity has traditionally valued, qualities like compassion, intellect, culture, spirituality, and they are unambiguously devoted to the violent destruction of our kind. They are also hive creatures, without a sepa-rate, individual existence. For readers who share Heinlein's right-wing libertarian politics, especially those readers of the 1950s or 1960s, they are easily read as a straightforward code for 'communists'. For many women, SF that writes this sort of opposition is too facile. In a discussion of the novels of Gwyneth Jones and Octavia Butler, Wolmark observes:

> The science fiction convention of the alien attempts to present other-ness in unitary terms, so that 'humanity' is uncomplicatedly opposed to the 'alien'; both Jones and Butler focus on the way in which the opposition seeks to suppress the others of both gender and race by subsuming them within a common-sense notion of what it is to be human.
>
> (Wolmark 1994: 46)

This complexity goes deeper than might at first be thought. Very little SF, even in the depths of male-authored Pulps, advances a 'common-sense notion of what it is to be human', and consequently representations of the 'alien' are very rarely as straightforwardly demonised as Heinlein's repulsive insect foe from *Starship Troopers*. Most aliens embody some degree of awareness of difference, which might be encoded in various ways, such as race, culture or gender.

An example of the encoding of gender might be found in the *Alien* films. This is a series that has become increasingly identified with one of its female characters, Ripley, as played by Sigourney Weaver. Ripley is a 'strong' woman in all four films, self-reliant and motivated to survive. Each of the four films shares the same basic premise: the encounter with a monstrous other, an alien who kills and mutilates. The gender identity of this beast seems straightforward enough: in the first film, *Alien*, it is an aggressive male, attacking and killing, penetrating its victims in a violent coding of rape with a monstrous toothed phallus that protrudes from its mouth. This same 'male' also impregnates some of its victims, placing a baby alien in their bellies, be they male or female, a symbolic death-fetus that is born by fatally bursting through the torso. But as the series progresses, this gender identification becomes problematised, partly through an identification with Ripley herself, such that the alien becomes a more extreme version of the woman. Ripley is tall and strong, but the alien is taller and stronger; Ripley survives in a series of ingenious ways, the alien survives more extreme threats. For instance, in *Aliens*, the second film, it survives even hanging outside a spacecraft in space. In *Aliens* Ripley is maternal, protecting 'Newt', a little girl who is the sole survivor of the alien attack; but the queen alien whom Ripley confronts is even more maternal, with a nest of 'thousands' of children, or eggs, which Ripley must try to destroy. Indeed, some critics argue that the alien, despite its various 'masculine' attributes, is representative throughout the films of 'the monstrous feminine'. Barbara Creed, for instance, points out that in *Alien* 'virtually all aspects of the *mise-en-scène* are designed to signify the female: womb-like interiors, fallopian tube corridors, small claustrophobic spaces', going on to argue that in contemporary culture 'the body, particularly the woman's body, has come to signify the unknown, the terrifying, the monstrous' (in Kuhn 1990: 215–16). By the third film, the identification of alien with woman, and of Ripley with alien, is becoming more explicit. 'The Bitch Is Back' announced the poster publicity for this film, over a double shot of Ripley and the alien confronting one another, the slogan apparently referring to either, or both, of them. By *Alien 4* Ripley and the alien have literally become one; reconstructed from contaminated DNA, Ripley becomes a woman–alien hybrid. In all of these films there is an acute turning away from men; all the men die in the first film, although Ripley is able to save the cat; all but one die in the second (and he dies shortly after), although Ripley does save the small girl; in the third film men are represented exclusively by criminals, rapists and outcasts, all but one of whom are killed; by the fourth movie the Ripley–alien struggles to save the life of the only other survivor from two separate spacecraft: a female android. There is a balance of horror and delight in the man-killing actions of the alien, both visceral distaste for the bloodshed and a certain admiration for the beauty and form of the alien itself, its instinctual ingenuity, its grace. It is a sort of aggressive compensatory fantasy, a woman who rapes but cannot be raped: if penetrated, the alien spurts disfiguring acid, something that wounds many characters in the films – all of whom are men.

From the point of view of gender representation, the effect of these four extremely popular films taken together is the strength given to positive representations of the female by so monstrous an embodiment of alterity as the alien monster it(her)self. The identification of the monster with 'femaleness' inverts some of the traditional sexist assumptions about what women are like. It is strong, violent, active rather than passive, and the fetishisation of that very monster, evidenced for instance by fannish obsession with the H. R. Geiger designs that shaped it, celebrates the bursting of traditional bounds. The *Alien* films eventually reveal themselves as being about hybridisation, with the Ripley/alien dual creature the only surviving organism, about to reach Earth and presumably spread her radically different DNA over the planet.

This celebration of the hybrid is one of the main strands of strong female SF, and in part it provides a direct access to the poetics of alterity. Sheri Tepper's novel *Grass* (1989) sets itself up as a sort of futuristic fairy tale. Conventional wife and mother Marjorie Westriding goes with her husband and children to the planet Grass in search of a cure for a devastating galactic plague. There she encounters an aristocratic culture dedicated to hunting foxes, except that the 'foxen' they hunt are actually enormous alien monsters that provide no clear outline to the eye but give a terrifying impression of claws and teeth. The 'horses' ridden by the human settlers are alien too, the Hippae, muscular and sharp-toothed. As the novel progresses, it becomes apparent that it is the Hippae who are ruling the occasion, telepathically compelling the human riders to help them hunt down and kill their enemies, the foxen. The human interest of the narrative traces out a story where, like a good feminist heroine, Westriding rebels against the strictness of her religious upbringing and turns against her husband's infidelity. But it is the end of the novel that is most striking, and the place where the encounter with difference is most dramatically realised: Marjorie Westriding does not choose to fall in love with the handsome human alternatives to her husband, nor to live independently (a common motif in feminist fiction), but instead falls in love with one of the foxen and rides away on him through an interdimensional portal. It is 'Beauty and the Beast', except that the beast not only remains a beast at the end of the tale, but it is his very bestiality, his irreducible otherness, that is the reason she falls in love with him. As Marleen Barr puts it: 'Marjorie learns that her ultimate emotional experience involves loving foxen while she is located outside patriarchy, not hunting them to prove her manhood. She chooses to love a male other to manhood whose species is persecuted in the name of proving manhood. She experiences splendour in the grass with an alien' (Barr 1987: 132).

Critic and theorist Donna Harraway has written an influential essay that celebrates exactly the feminist potential of this sort of hybridisation, focused for her by the figure of the cyborg. Part organic, part machine, the cyborg has been a common theme in SF for many decades. More often than not, SF cyborgs are menacing, like the Daleks of *Dr Who* or the Borg of *Star Trek*. By reclaiming the trope of the cyborg as a feminist icon, Harraway is perfectly aware that she is being controversial or, as she puts it, 'ironic' and 'blasphemous'. But her celebration of the feminist possibilities of the hybridisation of the cyborg has struck a chord with many thinkers, and not only feminist ones. Her point is initially that, as human beings who rely on machinery to an intimate and unprecedented degree, we (she is addressing herself to women) are already cyborgs, that 'the boundary between science fiction and social reality is an optical illusion' because 'the cyborg is a matter of fiction and lived experience that changes what counts as women's experience in the late twentieth-century' (Harraway 1991: 149). Her examples begin with real life, the commonplace cyborgs created by medicine, production, war and everyday life. The 'I' that is addressing you now, for instance, is only able to do so as a cyborg amalgamation of my flesh and the various machineries of computing, book production and distribution. Harraway then moves seamlessly on to the representation of cyborgs in science fiction, in which a variety of (mostly) female authors is lauded for creating 'a myth about identity and boundaries which might inform late twentieth-century political imaginations' (Harraway 1991: 173). It is the range of her examples as much as anything that is so significant: from the high feminist art of Joanna Russ's *The Female Man* to the complex highbrow Science Fantasy of Samuel Delany's *Nevèrÿon* sequence, to the right-wing Hard SF of John Varley and the popular writing of Anne McCaffrey. The books in Varley's trilogy, *Titan*, *Wizard* and *Demon*, are all set aboard an enormous part-organic part- technological space station/world in the shape of an enormous wheel orbiting Jupiter. McCaffrey's *The Ship Who Sang* (1969) is about a disabled girl whose mind is transferred into a spaceship. It is the diversity of this list of examples that is its point as much as anything. The cyborg may be monstrous, in the same way that the Alien is monstrous, or magnificent; but the crucial thing about it is that it is the site of the encounter with difference. In the words of Jane Donawerth, 'stories of alien women in science fiction by women thus take on, unmetaphor, and live out the cultural stereotypes of women. In each case, the narratives confront and transform the stereotypes' (Donawerth 1997: 107–8). This process of 'unmetaphoring', of unpacking and making explicit the metaphors by which stereotypes work, is exactly the strength of SF as a materialist mode of writing. Instead of presenting woman as a metaphorical alien in contemporary society, an SF text can present an *actual* woman (like Ripley) as an *actual* alien, can attack the stereotype in a more direct, more vivid and more powerful manner.

CASE STUDY: URSULA LE GUIN, *THE LEFT HAND OF DARKNESS* (1969)

Few works of SF, or of any literature, explore questions of gender as profoundly as Le Guin's masterpiece *The Left Hand of Darkness* (1969). The plot of Le Guin's novel is easily summarised. Genly Ai is an ambassador from the Hainish Ekumensis, who has come by himself to the world of Gethen, also known as Winter, with the aim of introducing that world to the spacefaring cultures of his interstellar commonwealth. Such ambassadors come alone, in order not to intimidate the home culture. Genly Ai comes first of all to the nation of Karhide, where he is befriended by the prime minister Estraven; but Karhide's king is mad and more than a little paranoid. He banishes Estraven for treason and rejects Genly Ai's mission. Genly then leaves Karhide and travels to the neighbouring nation of Orgoreyn, moving from a 'Western'-style culture to an Iron Curtain-vintage Eastern European one, a state bureaucracy, the second of the two superpowers of Gethen. Estraven has also fled here, and he and Genly Ai meet up again. Although the Orgoreyns seem initially favourable to Genly's mission, their thoughts are actually on an impending war with their neighbouring country. Genly and Estraven are thrown into a Siberian-style prison; they escape and embark on a huge trek across the winter ice-deserts, slowly and heroically making their way through appalling conditions back to Karhide on the other side of the world. At the end of this trek Estraven is killed, but Genly Ai makes it back to find the king now favourably disposed to his mission. The novel ends with Gethen, Winter, accepting further representations from the Ekumensis.

Critical attention on this novel has concentrated less on this storyline and more on the novel's premise. But in fact it is more correct to talk of the novel's two premises. The first is the climactic premise; Le Guin has imagined a world perennially stuck in winter. This is a winter planet, in the way that Herbert's *Dune* is a desert planet. On this planet it is cold during summer, and the winters plunge the world into astonishing snowstorms and lows of temperature. It is difficult to avoid the sense that everything that happens on Gethen is primarily shaped by the weather. Society has evolved out of close-knit communities called Hearths, partly familial, partly tribal, where people gather together against the cold. Everything from the architecture to the religion reflects the constraints of the weather. As Genly says himself, 'Winter is an inimical world; its punishment for doing wrong is sure and prompt.' Expulsion from the Hearths leads to 'death from cold, death from hunger' (Le Guin, *The Left Hand of Darkness* (1969): 88). The resulting society is close knit and regulated by complex social codes of 'face' or 'honour', *shifgrethor* as it is called.

But it is the second premise of the novel that has attracted the most critical attention, and that has the most obvious feminist implications. The world of Gethen, or Winter, has no fixed gender; nobody on this planet is 'male' or 'female'. Instead, all Gethenians live according to a monthly cycle. For most of this cycle they are neither male nor female, but sexless, or genderless, human beings. The technical term for this is androgyny, although the word implies being both sexually male and female, and this is not strictly the situation. For most of their lives Gethenians are neither male nor female. Once a month or so they enter a period called kemmer.

> In the first phase of kemmer, the individual remains completely androgynous. Gender, and potency, are not achieved in isolation ... Yet the sexual impulse is tremendously strong in this phase, control-ling the entire personality ... When the individual finds a partner in kemmer, hormonal secretion is further stimulated ... until in one partner either a male or female hormonal dominance is established. The genitals engorge or shrink accordingly, foreplay intensifies, and the partner, triggered by the change, takes on the other sexual role ... Normal individuals have no predisposition to either sexual role in kemmer; they do not know whether they will be the male or the female, and have no choice in the matter ... [Kemmer] ends fairly abruptly, and if conception has not taken place, the individual returns to the latent phase and the cycle begins anew. If the individ-ual was in the female role and was impregnated, hormonal activity of course continues, and for the gestation period the individual remains female ... With the cessation of lactation the female becomes once more a perfect androgyne. No physiological habit is established, and the mother of several children may be the father of several more.
>
> (Le Guin, *The Left Hand of Darkness* (1969): 82–3)

In her 1976 essay 'Is Gender Necessary?', a meditation upon her novel, Le Guin ponders 'why did I invent these peculiar people? Not just so that the book could contain, halfway through it, the sentence: 'the king was pregnant' – although I admit I am fond of that sentence' (Le Guin 1989: 137). The sentence seems to capture the point of the experiment; it contradicts our assumptions. Kings do not get pregnant, partly because they are male, and men do not have the physiological capacity for pregnancy, but also because a 'king' is an icon of masculine power, and it somehow diminishes our conception of that power to imagine it subject to the physical change of pregnancy.

In other words, in *The Left Hand of Darkness* Le Guin has hit upon a means of exploring the ways that gender and our assumptions about gender shape the world we live in. In a sense this is the fundamental feminist project: not a raising up of women at the expense of men, but a trying to see beyond the mystifications of gender-related ideology. Try this thought experiment: how greatly does the sex of the person you are talking to, or living with, or watching on television, determine the ways you respond? How might a world without gender work? Chapter 7 of Le Guin's novel is called 'The Question of Sex' and pinpoints some of the answers to these sorts of question.

> Anyone can turn his hand to anything. This sounds very simple, but its psychological effects are incalculable. The fact that everyone between seventeen and thirty-five or so is liable to be … 'tied down to childbearing', implies that no one is quite so thoroughly 'tied down' here as women, elsewhere, are likely to be – psychologically and physically.
>
> … A child has no pyscho-sexual relationship to his mother and father. There is no myth of Oedipus on Winter.
>
> … There is no division of humanity into strong and weak halves, protected/protective, dominant/submissive, owner/chattel, active/passive. In fact the whole tendency to dualism that pervades human thinking may be found to be lessened, or changed, on Winter.
>
> (Le Guin, *The Left Hand of Darkness* (1969): 84–5)

This last point is particularly interesting aesthetically. It is true that *The Left Hand of Darkness* is remarkably non-binary as a novel. This may be one reason why some critics like it so little. It is not an exaggeration to suggest that most of our literary tradition, certainly in the novel, has come out of a binary aesthetic. Texts are very frequently structured around binary oppositions such as 'good versus evil', as for example in Milton's *Paradise Lost* or the novels of Dickens. Indeed some critics (for instance, Harold Bloom in his book *Agon*) have argued that such binarism, or more specifically the conflict inherent in such opposition, is the root of the energy and appeal of literature. According to this model, Le Guin's text is something out of the ordinary. The novel contains little narrative tension, for instance. The larger question of whether Winter will join the Ekumensis is short-circuited early on in the book, when Genly Ai consults a Gethenian oracle and asks precisely that question. He is answered 'yes', and so it transpires. Predicting the future is not a matter of guesswork on Winter but is rather a certainty. This does not, however, function in Gethenian culture as a Pandoran curse. The oracles are calm, as are most people on this world. Genly Ai tries to put across to one of these future-tellers how startling this is to him.

> 'Faxe, tell me this. You Handdarata have a gift that men on every world have craved. You have it. You can predict the future. And yet you live like the rest of us – it doesn't seem to *matter* –'
> 'Why should it matter, Genry?'
>
> (Le Guin, *The Left Hand of Darkness* (1969): 64)

Genly is always coming across the Karhide verbal shrug-of-the-shoulders, 'nusuth', a word which means 'what does it matter?' or 'it doesn't matter'. It is as if, without the tension of fixed gender, the inhabitants of this world have achieved a greater degree of Zen-like acceptance about the cosmos. Although *The Left Hand of Darkness* is essentially the tale of two characters, Genly Ai, from offworld, and the native Estraven, and although we might assume they are very different beings from entirely different backgrounds, in fact Genly and Estraven seem very similar. The book tells the story of their bonding, their closeness, and the sorrow of Genly at Estraven's death. Their cultures may be different, but their individuality doesn't seem to be. On a larger level, the work is structured about two cultures, the 'Western' Karhide and the 'Eastern' Orgoreyn, and here the differences are apparently fairly pronounced. But because Winter society is rooted not in any notion of nationhood, something which is consistently shown to be a recent development in this ancient culture, but more in the Hearth, the individual relations between people, there is precious little tension here either. Le Guin herself has said that one of the initial impulses to write this novel came out of a desire to write a world that knew nothing of war.

> At the very inception of the whole book, I was interested in writing a novel about people in a society that had never had a war. That came first. The androgyny came second. (Cause and effect? Effect and cause?)
>
> (Le Guin 1989: 141)

Le Guin suggests that the warlessness of Winter is possibly the ultimate function of a genderless society, and by implication that war is nothing but a result of the fixed-gender nature of our own world. An interesting notion this, but, it might be argued, perhaps aesthetically deadening. War, as the apotheosis, has been the engine of literature at least since the *Iliad*. But this is precisely what makes *The Left Hand of Darkness* such an expert performance: it achieves its gripping, finely detailed vision of alterity without resorting to over-obvious tactics of narrative or character opposition.

On the other hand, Le Guin's 'genderless' conception of the world has come in for some fierce criticism, particularly from feminist writers. The brunt of this criticism has to do with her project of the elimination of gender: it is not that there is no gender on Winter, it is that there are no *women* on Winter. In part this has to do with the vexed question of the non-specific pronoun. Characters throughout the novel are called 'he'; the 'he/him/his' bias of the narrative is something Le Guin herself has subsequently regretted. She acknowledges that 'the Gethenians seem like men, instead of menwomen'. In her 1976 essay on the book she explained: 'I call the Gethenians "he" because I utterly refuse to mangle English by inventing a pronoun for "he/she".' Her 1987 revision of this essay backtracks: 'This "utter refusal" of 1968 restated in 1976 collapsed, utterly, within a couple of years more. I still dislike invented pronouns, but now dislike them less than the so-called generic pronoun "he/him/his", which does in fact exclude women from discourse; and which was an invention of male grammarians in the sixteenth century' (Le Guin 1989: 145).

Perhaps Le Guin is being unnecessarily hard on herself. If the Gethenians are portrayed largely as male, this has surely to do with the perspective of the male Genly Ai, which in turn says less about Winter and more about genderist assumptions from outside the world. Genly is narrator; it is Genly who chooses to call the monarch 'king'. The novel begins with an elaborately described procession, full of pomp and the rituals of power, and all is described in terms of the 'male' gender: king, men, lords, mayors and so on. At one point, Estraven invites Genly to supper as part of the complex power games of the city. Genly tells us he was 'annoyed by this sense of effeminate intrigue' (*Left Hand*, p. 14). Within a few pages, the narrator (not the author) has set up a pattern of good/bad, male/female binarisms. But one of the subtleties of the novel is to unravel the common preconceptions that power is somehow masculine and that relationships are somehow feminine. Estraven seems unambiguously a man: 'one of the most powerful men in the country ... He is lord of a Domain and lord of the Kingdom, a mover of great events' (p. 12). The king, in the impressive march of Chapter 1, is described in masculine terms. But by Chapter 3, when the king's paranoia becomes clearer, Genly's audience with him sees a shifting of gender. 'Agraven was less kingly, less manly, than he looked at a distance among his courtiers ... He laughed shrilly like an angry woman pretending to be amused' (p. 33). In this case, the negative associations of the adjectives connect with a common discourse that sees madness, or hysteria, as something more female than male. But the striking first sentence of Chapter 5, 'My landlady, a voluble man ... ' helps isolate the fact that the sexism here is Genly's, not the author's. The 'landlady' is a father not a mother, but Genly jumps to gender conclusions even when they flatly contradict the physical facts. 'He was so feminine in looks and manner that I once asked him how many children he had. He looked glum. He had never borne any. He had, however, sired four' (p. 47). By the time we have followed the narrative through to Genly and Estraven's heroic trek across the ice, questions of gender have largely been bleached from the novel. Estraven actually goes into kemmer during this journey, and since Genly is permanently male (a 'pervert' in Gethenian terms), this means Estraven is a 'she'. Certainly by its closing pages *The Left Hand of Darkness* has become a sort of inter-racial love story, but one of the beauties of this is that we are left uncertain about whether to read the unconsummated love between Genly and Estraven as homosexual or heterosexual.

In 'Is Gender Necessary?' Le Guin admits that 'one does not see Estraven as a mother, with his children, in any role that we automatically perceive as "female": and therefore, we tend to see him as a man. This is a real flaw in the book, and I can only be very grateful to those readers, men and women, whose willingness to participate in the experiment led them to fill in that omission with the work of their own imagination' (Le Guin 1989: 146). This is crucial, I think; one of the reasons *The Left Hand of Darkness* works so well is precisely that the creation of this imaginary world is so detailed and so compelling that readers are prompted to enter into the experiment fully. But in 1987 this position no longer satisfied Le Guin. She argued:

> I now see it thus: Men were inclined to be satisfied with the book, which allowed them a safe trip into androgyny and back from a conventionally male viewpoint. But many women wanted it to go further, to dare more, to explore androgyny from a woman's point of view as well as a man's ... I think women were justified in asking more courage of me and a more rigorous thinking-through of implications.
>
> (Le Guin 1989: 146)

But it might be better to represent the splitting of gender as working in a slightly different way. Joanna Russ sees Winter as being a community of men without women; we might with equal justification see it as a community of women without men. After all, the Gethenians are subject to a monthly cycle, as women are; all are liable to become pregnant and none of them have external genitalia. Estraven notes of the male Genly: 'there is a frailty about him. He is all unprotected, exposed, vulnerable, even to his sexual organ which he must carry always outside himself' (*Left Hand*, p. 194). When Genly tries to comprehend their society, he mostly reaches for female metaphors. The Hearth is a local group, like a family, which is supportive, nurturing. 'On Gethen', Genly observes, 'nothing led to war. Quarrels, murders, feuds, forays ... They lacked, it seemed, the capacity to mobilize. They behaved like animals in this respect, or women. They did not behave like men, or ants' (p. 47). The masculine element in the equation is the weather, comprised of vicious, sometimes hellish winter storms and wastelands through which Estraven and Genly battle in the latter sections of the novel.

The question that needs addressing, perhaps, is whether *The Left Hand of Darkness*'s twin premises can be aesthetically connected. Why does it follow that a book about a society without gender must also be a book about a society that lives in a perpetual winter? Several answers suggest themselves. Gwyneth Jones thinks that the icescapes of the novel reflect the intrusion into the centre of the narrative of the only man, Genly Ai, as if the novel is saying 'to become a woman is to *lose face*, to lose persona; to give up the role of the protagonist. This loss ... is the blank ice' of the novel's world (Jones 1999: 205). Alternatively, perhaps Le Guin instinctively sought a landscape of ice and waste to dramatise a society without change, without flux. The necessary corollary of the Gethenian warlessness is a resistance to change; this is a society that has reached levels of technology equivalent to that of our 1960s, but has failed to advance beyond it: 'the mechanical–industrial Age of Invention in Karhide is at least three thousand years old' (*Left Hand*, p. 31). There is no war, and accordingly there is no progress. In 'Is Gender Necessary?' Le Guin even talks of this as one of the positive aspects of the society:

> The Gethenians [lacking 'masculinity'] do not rape their world. They have developed a high technology, heavy industry, automobiles, radios, explosives, etc., but they have done so very slowly, absorbing their technology rather than letting it overwhelm them. They have no myth of progress at all.
>
> (Le Guin 1989: 141)

Le Guin casts this as a function of gender, but it might be possible to see it as being part of a broader science-fictional suspicion of technology, the nostalgic, backward-looking machine phobia that has informed almost all the books we have looked at. But Le Guin's artistry is more than her ideology. There is something appealing about the world of Gethen, but there is something stagnant there too. As we learn right at the beginning, the Gethenians have no linear calendar, but reckon each year as Year One. 'It is always Year One here. Only the dating of every past and future year changes each New Year's day, as one counts backwards or forwards from the unitary Now' (*Left Hand*, p. 9).

That Le Guin manages to make this frozen society, this genderless social wasteland, so powerfully engaging is the great triumph of her art. And I think it has to do with the way she harks back to a far older culture than most SF. The interspersed tales from Gethenian folklore are examples of the oldest form of discourse there is, oral tales. Estraven tells an audience:

> The whole tale of our crossing the ice. He told it as only a person of an oral-literature tradition can tell a story, so it became a saga, full of traditional locations and even episodes, yet exact and vivid, from the sulphurous fire and dark of the pass between Drumner and Dremegole to the screaming gusts from mountain-gaps that swept the bay of Guthen.
>
> (Le Guin, *The Left Hand of Darkness* (1969): 232)

Le Guin conveys her own story not as if she is inventing a new narrative, but as if she is relating an ancient tale. In the frequently tech-obsessed narratives of much twentieth-century SF this is a radical and empowering form of formal difference.

Hand in hand with this goes Le Guin's spirituality. Like 'the Force' in the equally mythic-aesthetic *Star Wars* or the Bene Gesserit Sisterhood in Herbert's *Dune*, there is a strand of mysticism running throughout the otherwise rationalist fabric of the text. As has been mentioned, the Gethenians are able to tell the future; prophets live in ascetic hermitages deep in the ice, one of which Genly visits. All the Gethenians he meets have an almost Buddhist acceptance of karma. It even filters down to the level of Le Guin's imagery, which is always concise and economical, and always effective. A Karhide town has houses with 'roofs pitched steep as praying hands' (Left Hand, p. 101). This is a fine image, both practical – the roofs are built that way so as not to accumulate snow during the heavy winter storms – and symbolic, a relation of the immanent Gethenian spirituality. This, it seems to me, is why *The Left Hand of Darkness* is set in the landscape it occupies: barrenness is the appropriate environment for spirituality, because it focuses attention on the spirit rather than on the body. And by the same token, Le Guin's genderless world points in the same direction and prompts us to the same conclusion: that without the sexual distractions of gender, always referring us back to our corporeality, we too could acquire a more spiritual outlook on life.

4

SF AND RACE

Race is a key concern of a great deal of contemporary SF. Indeed, it should not surprise us that a genre fascinated by the encounter with difference should have so often dramatised the various encounters of racial difference that have done so much to shape twentieth-century culture, from the civil rights movements of the 1960s and the explosion of black cultural expression of the 1960s and 1970s, through to the multicultural present day.

This is, however, more than a simple matter of coding 'the alien' as black, although it sometimes is this. One of the strengths of science fiction is that it allows for a more complex and sophisticated response to the dynamics of difference, as well as allowing these issues to be addressed in a popular idiom. This chapter sets out to discuss aspects of the representation of blackness in SF, although this is more than merely a matter of identifying black characters in SF novels. Having a black protagonist may be central to what a novel is trying to do, as in Octavia Butler's superb, if harrowing, *Kindred* (1979), or it may be a purely incidental feature, something not rendered in terms of racial difference at all, or dropped casually into the novel to suggest how far removed its future-world is from the divisions of racial disharmony today; for instance, the protagonist of Robert Heinlein's *Starship Troopers* (1959) is Fillipino, although little is made of this feature in the book. Altering the racial identity of the hero to Aryan in Verhoeven's 1997 film of the book went some way towards producing a more straightforwardly fascist text. This is not the point. The encounter with racial difference, and the profound impact of the black diaspora, have shaped twentieth-century American culture. SF reflects this impact, something it cannot do simply by playing around with protagonists' skin colours. Rendering the diversity of these mutual encounters in their beauty and possibility as well as their violence and bigotry requires a more complex fictive response.

This chapter will examine some of the ways 'blackness' has signified in SF by looking at two highly regarded authors who are black, Samuel Delany and Octavia Butler, as well as the ways SF has influenced other aspects of black and general popular culture. Various texts have used 'space alien' or 'robot' as a straightforward coding for blackness, but the more interesting representations make complex what can be a straightforward demonisation. Ridley Scott's *Alien* (1979) represents the alien as a black-skinned monster, played, in the original film, by a black actor in a suit, who lurks in the bowels of the industrial ship, a symbol of the industrial city, killing via a ghastly combination of rape and violence. It doesn't take much cultural decoding to see this as an expression of white middle-class fear at the potential for distrust of an alienated black urban underclass. In John McTiernan's *Predator* (1987) the savage hunter alien has dreadlocks, a clear enough signifier of blackness. He inhabits the jungle, preying violently and barbarically on the 'Western' colonisers, be they American, 'Dutch' or Hispanic. He also, when he finally uncovers his face at the end of the movie, has a peculiar mouth with teeth that look like bones pierced through his face: another 'jungle man' caricature of racial blackness. The coding is made even more explicit in the sequel, when the action relocates from the jungle to the urban battlefield of Los Angeles, another, more politically loaded location for white fears of black violence, with the alien joining in the gang war. In the first film the *Predator* is destroyed by the Aryan übermann Arnold Schwarzenegger. In the second the casting is even more ingenious: the black actor Danny Glover is pitted against the black-man-as-alien, precisely in the scene where black-on-black violence in contemporary America is at its most acute.

But the SF embodiment of 'black man or woman as alien' need not be as crude as this. For a great many writers, not least black SF authors, exploring the life of the alien becomes a supple and effective way of extrapolating their own positions as alienated individuals. This is the point that Marleen Barr makes when she points out that 'women – especially black women – who are alien in relation to patriarchal society, alter fiction's depiction of the alien' (Barr 1987: 98). Barr's own example, Octavia Butler's *Xenogenesis* trilogy, manages to create alien species that are genuine in their otherness without reducing them to the discourse of violent threat, although Butler is very precise when it comes to delineating the human terror and violence in the face of the radically strange. But there are many other examples of works that detail otherness in a fertile conjunction with blackness, that do so with subtlety and suggestiveness, and in a popular idiom.

REPRESENTING RACE

Representing blackness, then, is not simply a question of representing black characters or black protagonists in SF texts, not even of representing black characters as empowered, attractive and suchlike. If such representation is not contextualised politically, then it can be something incidental, something not to do with the encounter with difference in any meaningful way. I mentioned Heinlein's black protagonist in *Starship Troopers*; we might also point to the protagonist of Ursula Le Guin's *The Left Hand of Darkness*. Genly Ai is a black man, a fact mentioned, by the way, as being unimportant in itself during the course of the fiction. Whilst this reflects positively upon the relative lack of bigotry of Le Guin's imaginary gender-free society, it perhaps runs the risk of simply obscuring issues of racial difference. In Michael Moorcock's *A Cure for Cancer* (1971) the protean hero Jerry Cornelius is black (he's white in other novels), but the point of such a racial identity was rather lost in the psychedelic swirl of the 1960s surrealism of those books, unless the point of Jerry's being black was exactly to add an exotic, bohemian edge to the novels, in which case 'blackness' was being deployed wholly from the point of view of a limited white perspective. 'Black' does not connote 'exotic, bohemian otherness', if you happen to be black and brought up in a black environment. More edged is Moorcock's representation of the charismatic black dictator who conquers America in his novel *The Land Leviathan* (1974). As a dictator,

Hood commits crimes of oppression and war particularly against whites, but he is always articulate and intelligent when talking about his actions and his motivations, and the novel presents him as paradoxical, never endorsing his violence but never condemning him outright either, aware of the centuries of violence against blacks that constitute American history, against which Hood is only reacting. *The Land Leviathan* is less of a novel than any of the 'Jerry Cornelius' books (it is perfunctory in conception, short, baldly written), but as a text about race it at least avoids presenting race as a hidden issue, something hardly worth talking about.

Samuel Delany, himself a black SF writer and critic, has made a similar point when asked to comment on the Rastafarian characters in William Gibson's celebrated *Neuromancer* (1984). Some critics have seen Gibson's Rastas as a positive racial representation that reflects well on the novel as a whole, a novel, we might argue, that is particularly aware of the varieties of difference. The Rastas live in a jury-rigged orbital colony where they can follow their religion, and their music, in peace; they keep themselves to themselves, although they are not averse to helping Case and his colleagues in their campaign against the international capitalist edifice of Tessier-Ashpool; they are a positive representation, we might think, of strong, ideologically sound, self-reliant otherness. Delany sees it differently. However much he admires the novel as a whole, he sees Gibson's Rastas as too passive to dramatise the tensions of racial difference effectively; they are 'computer illiterates', 'women are not part of the rasta colony at all', they are presented as being easily manipulated by the sinister Artificial Intelligence, Wintermute. 'As a black reader', he has said, he finds it difficult to applaud 'this passing representation of a powerless and wholly non-oppositional set of black dropouts by a Virginia-born white writer' (Delany in Dery 1993: 751). By way of contrast, Delany cites a very different text, Robert Heinlein's *Farnham's Freehold* (1964). In that novel, Hugh Farnham, a right-wing white patriarch from the 1960s, is taking refuge in his personal bunker with his family and a black manservant called Joseph, when the whole caboodle is jolted forward in time by a nuclear war. They emerge to an America in which blacks are in charge and whites are enslaved and used as objects of sexual attraction or even as food. It might seem, on the surface, that this unpleasant story is nothing short of racist. Heinlein's novel might well be thought of as dramatising middle-class white anxieties about the American black underclass ('if we give them the chance, they'll turn on us and devour us'). But Delany insists that, because this is a novel that dramatises racial difference in terms of conflict, because its very extremism makes us think, it functions as a better book 'about' race:

> Though I doubt that [many readers] would approve of the course or outcome of Heinlein's story, the point is that Joseph is articulate, he has real power, and Heinlein is consciously ironizing powerful cultural myths of cannibalism precisely for their troubling anxieties. He forces us, in the course of his tale, to think through the situation – even if we don't agree with him, or his mouthpiece, Hugh Farnham.
>
> (Delany in Dery 1993: 752)

For Delany the moral seems to be that an SF novel needs to aim not at political correctness, or at an unspoken decency regarding race; instead it should make us think about these issues, confront us with them, as only a literature of ideas can. Certainly, Delany's own work has been fascinated with the complex interactions between cultures and races from the beginning. One of his most famous novels, *The Einstein Intersection* (1968), is a brief but immensely fertile and suggestive fable on the workings of difference. As Damien Broderick puts it, 'from his earliest fictions ... Samuel Delany has followed the vocation of what we might call "allographer", one who writes the Other' (Broderick 1995: 117).

In *The Einstein Intersection* Earth has been abandoned long ago by humanity and is now inhabited by a diverse range of mutated and exotic variations on the old 'human' model. Some of these mutations have produced striking and positive changes, from characters who can read minds or see the future to those who have increased strength and dexterity. At the other end of the scale, some mutations are so debilitating and deforming that those born with them must be sequestered, put in the 'kage'. As the protagonist, Lo Lobey (the 'Lo' as a forename signifies his masculinity, just as 'La' before a name signifies femaleness and 'Le' androgyny), travels from the countryside to the city, we realise that these posthumans are acting out the primal myths of their human predecessors, living in the ruins, as it were, of human culture. As one character puts it, 'we have taken over their abandoned world, and something new is happening to the fragments, something we can't even define with mankind's leftover vocabulary' (p. 131). Lo Lobey's story might be defined as a version of the ancient myth of Orpheus and Eurydice, or of Theseus and the Minotaur, or the more contemporary (to us) myth of Billy the Kid, but none of these narrative templates are adequate to describe what happens in this poetic, exotic, strange and beautiful little book. Indeed, this is Delany's whole point, that 'difference' is not something that can be completely apprehended by the vocabulary of sameness, that there is always going to be something beyond, which can't be expressed in the old language. This is why the tutelary spirit of the novel, as it were, is the twentieth-century mathematician Godel; the place where his Incompleteness theorem (of which the novel provides an artistic embodiment) intersects with the more rationalist Einsteinian physics provides the novel's title. 'Different' is a term that crops up again and again in the novel; it is the word used by characters to denote 'mutated', 'changed', 'possessing some ability that is outwith the range of the normal'. When Lobey reveals that he can read a character's mind, that character says 'you're different, aren't you?' (p. 75). But it is also used negatively, as a shorthand for the bigoted dismissal of otherness. In these terms, 'different' means merely 'freak' or 'deformed'. The positive and negative deployments of the discourse of difference, of course, have resonances with the debates about 'race' that have been so prominent in twentieth-century America.

Difference for Delany, it needs to be stressed, is about more than just race. In this novel, for instance, it becomes an almost universal artistic enabler, a means of opening up possibilities. But we can't ignore the fact that difference in Delany's hands is also about race. Lobey, for instance, introduces himself in self-deprecating terms that inevitably enter the discourse of race.

What do I look like?

Ugly and grinning most of the time. That's a whole lot of big nose and gray eyes and wide mouth crammed on a small brown face proper for a fox ... I have a figure like a bowling pin, thighs, calves, and feet of a man (gorilla?) twice my size (which is about five-nine)

> and hips to match. There was a rash of hermaphrodites the year I was
> born, which doctors thought I might be ... My feet have toes almost
> as long as my fingers, and the big ones are semi-opposable.
>
> (Delany, *Einstein Intersection* (1970): 7–8)

Delany is self-consciously playing with negative racial stereotypes here
and going some way towards reversing their associations. Lobey is a
musician; he has a hollow machete with holes down the blade: 'when I
blow across the mouthpiece in the handle, I make music with my blade'
(p. 1). Or to put it another way, he is an artist, like Delany himself.
That Lobey is gorilla-like, in the terms of this novel, means only that he
has a greater dexterity – he can, for instance, play his iconic musical
flute-sword with his fingers or his toes – as well as greater strength.
Delany also deliberately contrasts a certain rustic crudity (Lobey) with
the suave deadliness of the racially white Kid Death, with his red hair
and white skin ('his skin', says one character, 'was soap white').

Delany effectively introduces himself into the novel via Lobey (a self-
referential cypher) as well as quoting extensively from his own authorial
journals as chapter epigraphs. And there is a racial reason why it is Lobey
who destroys Kid Death at the novel's end and not the other way around.
In Delany's universe it is diversity and hybridity that are strength. 'To
survive even a dozen more generations,' says the novel's Jean Harlow/
Aphrodite figure, 'we must keep the genes mixing, mixing, mixing' (p.
146). Delany's own racially mixed heritage, his own diversely focused sexuality, his varied life and eclectic literary tastes all come together to produce him as an artist and to produce his art; and this is something he puts
unambiguously into his novel. Lobey is not just different because of a few
physical markers to do with his skin and physiognomy (which is to say,
different racially); his difference is something more profound. A random
mutation has given him the ability to hear the music in other people's
minds and to recreate it on his musical sword, has made him, in other
words, an artist. Kid Death is contemptuous of this ability:

> 'What power do you have?' Kid Death demanded. 'What can you do
> with your difference! Speak to a few deaf men, dead men, pierce the
> minds of a few idiots?'
>
> (Delany, *Einstein Intersection* (1970): 106)

But the force and beauty of this novel take its brown-skinned protagonist on a quest towards the core of what Art is, a quest that results in the destruction of Kid Death.

As a means of reclaiming 'difference' as a positive quantity, SF has provided many black writers and artists with the means to reconfigure prejudice. Nor is this confined to printed media. Kodwo Eshun's book *More Brilliant Than the Sun* (1998) has explored the black component of what he calls 'sonic fiction': the ways popular music has taken on the tropes and trappings of SF to express itself. The first rock star to fully explore SF was probably David Bowie; his 'Major Tom' character, followed by his persona as 'The Man Who Fell to Earth', found in SF an effortlessly effective carriage for the gender-bending otherworldly weirdness. 'Difference' here is predominantly gender and fits neatly into an imagined SF universe. But, as Eshun demonstrates, there were a great many black musicians drawn to the same fantastic strategies for locating their own notions of 'difference'. The prolific jazz-funk musician 'Sun-Ra' employed the vocabulary of space travel as a means of articulating racial difference in a positive manner in more than 100 albums, including *We Travel the Spaceways* (mid-1960s), *The Heliocentric Worlds of Sun Ra, Volume One* (1965) and *Sun-Ra and his Solar Arkestra Visits Planet Earth* (1966). More recently, various black hip-hop stars have matched the futuristic timbre of their techno-music with the iconography of SF. As Eshun suggests, part of the point of these sorts of artistic endeavour has been to distance black art from stereotypes. In music the most enduring of these stereotypes has been 'the Street', the sense that black music comes from and therefore necessarily must reflect a certain range of gritty urban realities. Refusing to conform to this caricature, and instead conceptualising black music as expansively fantastic, becomes a powerful artistic manoeuvre. Representation does not need to be chained to a limited notion of 'realism' to have powerful, realistic effects. Art can create a climate where the first associations of blackness are not 'Huggy Bear' (the shady black underworld character from *Starsky and Hutch*), but rather Geordi LaForge or Guinan from the starship *Enterprise*.

RACE AND STAR TREK

Some critics have analysed the original series of *Star Trek* in terms of its representation of race and find the show limited and even tacitly racist. In some senses, *Trek* might seem an odd target for anti-racist wrath. Gene Roddenberry was vocal about his desire to represent a future in which discrimination on grounds of race or gender was a thing of the past and was proud of the ethnically integrated bridge crew, with a white American captain, Japanese and Russian helm officers, a black woman communications officer and so on. But the apparent diversity of the crew was in fact subordinated to the white ideal represented by Kirk; Lieutenant Uhura (whose dialogue was often extremely limited and sometimes pared down to 'hailing frequencies open, Captain') was a marginal figure in many senses. The idea here is that the original series of *Star Trek* was a text of its time, and that representation of race was predicated upon a sense that 'whiteness' was the norm from which other races deviated (and to which other races might aspire). Supporters of the show point to its consistently applied liberal ethos, and the fact that many episodes directly addressed issues of race and racial discrimination. 'Let That Be Your Last Battlefield' is one example of this. Kirk and the crew come across a planet caught in a savage civil war between two different 'races'. The people of this planet are humanoid and divided into two colours by a line running down the middle of their faces and bodies (a rather harlequinesque colour scheme), with one side black and the other white. One portion of the population is *black* on the left side and *white* on the right, the other section is white on the left side and black on the right. Their mutual hatred strikes us as based on an especially arbitrary discrimination, and the message of the show, that racial conflict in our own time is similarly arbitrary, is unmistakable. Liberal fans of *Star Trek* might also point out that it often represented black characters in senior social positions (renowned doctors, senior officers), and that it was the first show on American TV to show an inter-racial kiss, between Kirk and Uhura. But this kiss is not actually as straightforward a gesture of racial equality as it appears. Although Kirk seems to spend almost every episode kissing one or other (white-skinned or in one case green-skinned) alien, so much so that a rather troglodyte version of 'command masculinity' is constructed by the show, his solitary kiss with a black-skinned woman is a fraught affair. He does not *want* to kiss Uhura, perhaps because she is one of his crew (although he has no problem desiring white-skinned members of his crew in other episodes), and she does not want to kiss him. They are both compelled to kiss by evil, mind-controlling aliens, who force this degrading and 'wrong' spectacle for their own entertainment. Overall, it is difficult to deny that 'blackness' in the original series of *Star Trek* is a marginalised quantity, and that 'whiteness' is not only normalised but represented as an ideal.

Later versions of *Trek* were more self-consciously integrated. One of the main characters in *Star Trek: the Next Generation* – Geordi – is played by LeVar Burton, another black actor. Burton played the character of Kunta Kinte in the extremely popular TV dramatisation of Alex Haley's *Roots* (1976), a show which constituted pretty much the first time many of the issues of racial discrimination and the appalling history of slavery were given an airing on national TV. Burton acquired a significant fan base amongst African-Americans (and others) on the back of this groundbreaking portrayal, and his decision to play Geordi in *Trek* took many of these fans with him. What seems to me to be positive about Burton's portrayal of Geordi is the way it resolutely refuses the stereotypical attributes of black manhood; Geordi is, basically, a supercompetent computer nerd, not a type usually represented by black characters. In the show, and especially in the early series, Geordi is extremely dedicated to his work, shy around women, with relatively poor social skills, and his best friend is a robot. He is also blind, a feature which occasionally elicits negative discrimination from others (as in the episode 'The Masterpiece Society'), although his skin colour never does. He is also, I should add, a very appealing character, a senior officer with real powers and responsibilities, and is given a great many feature episodes and important scenes. It is this sort of complex casting both with and against type that marks out a certain sophistication in Trek's representation of colour.

The Klingons make an interesting case study in the representation of 'race'. In the original series they were played by white actors and seemed, fairly straightforwardly, to connote 'orientalism', particularly a caricature of the Japanese. Their faces, hair and samurai costumes as much as their warrior society were particularly suggestive in America in the 1960s, a time when many Americans (Roddenberry included) had fresh memories of fighting the Japanese in the Second World War. As they appear in the original series, the Klingons are without redeeming qualities: they are brutish, devious, dangerous and murderous, the very embodiment of a racist demonisation of the oriental other. But for the cinematic adventures of the *Star Trek* crew, and then in *Star Trek: the Next Generation*, the Klingons are treated in a more sympathetic light. Although still violent and aggressive, the presence of Worf on the *Enterprise*, followed by a large number of episodes set amongst Klingon culture, fleshed out their way of life, making it seem much more attractive. Fans loved it, and a wide range of spin-offs from the series entered general circulation; the Klingon language, for instance, was invented fully enough for people to converse in it, and Klingon dictionaries and grammatical primers sold well. CD-ROMS giving more insight into the Klingon way were also popular, and as first *Star Trek: the Next Generation* and then *Star Trek: Deep Space Nine* devoted more time to Klingon characters and concerns, it became apparent that a race introduced in the original series as the Villains had become the Heroes.

This shift from villain status to hero status is marked, I think, by a revealing shift in the cultural sensibilities with which Klingons are apprehended. In short, this involves an internalisation of the cultural signifier 'Klingon' into a North American cultural logic, albeit one that still marks their separation. What I mean by this is that, from being coded as 'Japanese' (and therefore un-American), the Klingons became coded as African-American (almost all Klingon characters are now played by African-American actors), and more specifically as Native-American (the 'warrior culture' integral to Klingon life became less samurai and more Sioux, so that, for instance, the Klingon war-cry, 'Today is a good day to die!', is drawn from Sioux traditions). Whilst neither African-American nor Native-American represents the dominant cultural strand in current constructions of 'American-ness', they are both potent and significant narratives within that overall ideology. Villain (equal to 'un-American') had been made American as part of the process of recreating the Klingons as heroic.

Star Trek's approach to the questions of race, then, is not exactly utopian, but it does at least allow a space for debate, a significant role for black actors and characters and a certain utopian impulse that encourages viewers to think through problems of difference.

ALIEN ABDUCTION

Race, I have been suggesting, is something central to late twentieth-century Western culture, and America in particular. It shouldn't surprise us if race is so ubiquitous in American SF, something revealed not just in novels written from an SF perspective but also in culture in general.

The argument would go something like this: because race has been so important to postwar America, the myths and discourses of America tend to embody a consciousness of race. What, for instance, primarily distinguishes 'the space alien' from the human being? We might say any number of things (tentacles, bug-eyes, many arms, slime and so on), but the chances are we would agree on one thing: skin colour. Aliens, as popular consciousness knows, are differently coloured: green-skinned, blue-skinned or (more latterly) grey-skinned. Skin colour, in other words, is reflected by SF as the key vector of difference. TV shows such as *Alien Nation* (which was a spin-off from a popular film) posit the arrival of aliens from another world who settle amongst humanity to live and work like any other immigrants as the underclass of affluent America. Apart from a number of bizarre differences (the ability to get drunk on sour milk, being burnt by seawater as if by acid, and so on) the predominant difference between humans and these humanoid aliens is their skin colour; the aliens are patterned exotically, we might almost say in jungle colours. As SF writer Greg Tate points out, in *Alien Nation* the aliens 'were former slaves who were brought to earth on a ship and just dumped on these shores' (Tate in Dery 1993: 764). It seems almost too straightforward an SF allegory.

A show such as *The X-Files*, on the other hand, has little explicitly to say about race. But its dominant narrative fascination, that of alien abduction, is a revealing contemporary American myth. Studies put the number of Americans who literally believe in alien abduction in the millions, and a variety of critics have attempted to come to terms with why this story is so extraordinarily popular (see, for instance, Luckhurst 1998). One thing the alien abduction narrative does, as several critics have noted, is to retell the story of the African slave trade by relocating it to a contemporary SF context. The typical abductee is a white, moderately affluent thirty-something American. Abductees are taken suddenly from their homes by aliens, restrained (perhaps shackled) and transported to the alien spaceship. Once there they are subjected to physically degrading and sometimes painful treatment by aliens who seem callously indifferent to their suffering. Some of these treatments seem to involve some sort of 'tagging' (the insertion, for instance, of devices into nose or ear); some of them constitute sexual assault, such as the insertion of probes into genital or rectal areas, the stimulation of the penis and the removal of sperm, or the investigation of the womb. At the end of this process, the aliens compel the abductees to forget, or at least to suppress, memories of the experience, usually with some quasi-telepathic invasion of the mind. What happens with alien abduction, in other words, is what Freudians call 'the return of the repressed', although on a societal level. The brutal realities of the trade in slaves, which involved precisely the abduction of people from their homes, physical humiliation, violence and sexual assault, are intimately complicit with the history and indeed the success of America. Such narratives sit uncomfortably with the discourse of 'the land of the free' and have been largely and, until recently, successfully suppressed, to be replaced with stories of Pilgrim Fathers and intrepid wagon trains going west. But things do not disappear by being pushed down into the political unconscious, and the return of this violent, cruel and fundamentally American narrative manifests itself in a variety of new ways. In the case of alien abduction, mainstream America is fantasising a science-fictionalised version of eighteenth and nineteenth-century slaving and interpolating itself into the victim role. It is very much to do with race.

CASE STUDY: BUTLER'S *XENOGENESIS*

One of today's most highly regarded SF novelists, Octavia Butler, takes the alien abduction narrative as the starting point for her masterpiece, the *Xenogenesis* trilogy. In the first novel of this trilogy, *Dawn* (1987), Lilith Iyapo, a well-to-do African-American woman, wakes to find herself in a grey, enclosed room aboard a spaceship. She has no memory of how she came to be there and cannot explain the scar across her belly, something which seems to suggest invasive alien procedures. Interrogation by her alien captors is, in the first instance, an intimidating and sinister business: 'Her captors spoke when they were ready and not before. They did not show themselves at all. She remained sealed in her cubicle and their voices came to her from above like the light' (Butler, *Dawn* (1997): 5). Lilith remembers the nuclear war that had destroyed her world and remembers the death of her family.

As the novel continues, the aliens reveal themselves not to be malicious or sadistic, but instead benign and positive. They have rescued the remnants of humanity from the aftermath of nuclear conflict and have kept them unconscious on their orbiting spaceship for 250 years, until the Earth could be made habitable again. They intend to awaken this human population and release it back into the wild, as it were. In return they require only one thing from humanity: their genes. Butler's aliens, the Oankali, are essentially traders in genetic material, continually augmenting their own bodies with genetic diversity from other species, a process they can control at a molecular level. These aliens, then, are the symbolic embodiment of diversity. Their strength lies in the technology they wield, which is always represented in a suitably Edenic, utopian manner as *organic* technology, and their position as the literal saviours of mankind reflects that diversity as a fundamental good. Although they are not cartoonishly 'virtuous' (they do not always tell humans the truth about their plans, and they do sometimes force themselves upon humans), their balance of rational and generally kindly demeanour tends to valorise their cosmos-view. Diversity and hybridity are the absolute *raison-d'être* of these aliens: 'we do what you would call genetic engineering', one of them tells Lilith. 'We do it naturally. We *must* do it. It renews us, enables us to survive as an evolving species instead of specialising ourselves into extinction or stagnation' (p. 39). As a result of this, Butler's Oankali have a radically contrary approach to difference from that of most humans. In the second book of the trilogy Lilith says as much, talking to her son, a hybrid human–Oankali called Akin:

> 'Human beings fear difference,' Lilith had told him once. 'Oankali crave difference. Humans persecute their different ones, yet they need them to give themselves definition and status. Oankali seek difference

and collect it. They need it to keep themselves from stagnation and overspecialisation … When you feel a conflict [within yourself], try to go the Oankali way. Embrace difference.'

(Butler, *Adulthood Rites* (1997): 80)

That last sentence might stand as the epigraph for the whole *Xenogenesis* trilogy. It is interesting to contrast the Oankali, a race of aliens who cruise the galaxy seeking out new life in order to assimilate its difference to themselves, and who are not prepared to leave any unaltered human beings behind on Earth, with a similarly conceived race of aliens from *Star Trek*, the Borg. The Borg are thoroughly evil, conceived only in terms of threat, the most extreme of *Trek*'s demonisations of the alien as other. Butler's Oankali, on the other hand, constitute one of SF's most convincing utopian experiments, a profound and moving exploration of the possibilities alterity could bring with it.

This attempt at utopia is one strand of Butler's trilogy, but perhaps the books are more focused on the extreme difficulty all the humans have in the face of such radical difference. In the first volume Lilith undergoes a slow and painful process of acclimatisation to the strangeness of the aliens. Their skin, which is covered in sensory tentacles and feelers of varying sizes ('Medusa children. Snakes for hair. Nests of night crawlers for eyes and ears'), causes her the most problem (*Dawn*, p. 41). Even when she accepts the aliens and even takes an alien mate, the sheer weirdness of these phallic organs continues to bother her. That there is something sexual at the root of this *unheimlich* quality is made explicit both in their characterisation, and by the fact that Lilith and her human partner find a super-sexual bliss in conjunction with their mutual alien mate:

She tore off her jacket and seized the ugly, ugly elephant's trunk of an organ, letting it coil round her as she climbed onto the bed. She sandwiched Nikanj's [the alien's] body between her own and Joseph's.

(Butler, *Dawn* (1997): 161)

But it is the setting of a black woman at the core of this story that brings us back to issues of race. We discover that Lilith has been awakened by the Oankali for a particular reason: she is to 'parent' a group of newly awakened humans, to guide them into a position of acceptance of their new position. She doesn't want this job, but that is the very reason why she has been given it by the aliens: 'somebody who desperately doesn't want the responsibility, who doesn't want to lead, who is a woman' (*Dawn*, p. 157). In other words, as Jenny Wolmark puts it, this is a novel about the ways a character's 'marginality, articulated in terms of both gender and race, [can] become her strength' (Wolmark 1994: 32). As a black woman, Lilith might traditionally be represented as marginal, but Butler's SF context redefines the concept of the marginal with the hybrid space aliens in whose domain the story takes place.

5

SF AND TECHNOLOGY

Machines and technology are what we most associate with SF, just as we have now grown utterly accustomed to having a wide range of machines and technology surrounding us in our everyday lives. This might make it difficult for 'the machine' to figure alterity; but there can be little doubt that this is precisely the space occupied by the machine in the SF text.

We might think of high-tech machines as the necessary props of any SF tale. A novel may be in every salient regard a straightforward realist novel, but this straightforward realist content set on a spaceship travelling between the stars becomes science fiction. C. J. Cherryh's *Port Eternity* (1982) retells the legends of King Arthur aboard a spaceship, with robots playing the roles of knights and ladies; these two nova, the spaceship and the robot, are what relocates the story from Arthurian fantasy to SF. James Cameron's *Terminator* (1984) is Mary Shelley's *Frankenstein* revisioned via gleaming machines instead of body parts. A piece of futuristic, extrapolated technology is most often the technological novum that distinguishes a story as SF in the first place and is, therefore, more than merely a decorative addition to its narrative. More than this, it is the metaphorical effectiveness of technology in SF that focuses the SF encounter with alterity in its most suggestive locus. This is to say that a piece of SF technology, say a ray-gun, a spaceship, a time-machine or a matter-transporter, provides a direct, material embodiment of alterity; and that it is exactly because our lives are already surrounded by so many instances of near-miraculous technology, iPods, computers, TV, mobile phones, that this novum speaks so directly to us. Technology is something with which we are simultaneously familiar and already estranged from; familiar because it plays so large a part in our life, estranged from because we don't really know how it works or what the boffins are about to invent next.

Isolating the technological features from SF highlights the fact that in most cases technology works in science fiction either directly or obliquely to collapse together the machine and the organic. The bulk of SF technology articulates the trope of the cyborg, the machine/organic hybrid that is both a special instance of technology and the emblem for all of it. Readers of SF are organic, and the point of relevance of SF technology is that place where the machine intersects with the body. Scott Bukatman argues that '*the body* has long been the repressed content of science fiction, as the genre obsessively substitutes the rational for the corporeal, and the technological for the organic'. As Bukatman points out, nothing repressed stays repressed for very long, and SF texts have 'stage[d] the return of the repressed' by 'construct[ing] their own emphatic, techno-organic reconstructions of the flesh' (Bukatman 1993: 19). The ubiquitous technological trappings of SF, in other words, actually include within them the eruption of the body, of bodies like yours or mine, into the otherwise alienating discourse of the machine.

The key machines of SF are spaceships and robots/computers. The spaceship is almost always humanised; it may be sentient itself, like the frolicsome machines of Iain M Banks' *Culture* novels, from *Consider Phlebas* (1987) through to *Excession* (1997), or created by joining human and machine, as in Anne McCaffrey's *The Ship Who Sang* (1969), or controlled by a thinking machine like HAL in Arthur C Clarke's *2001: a Space Odyssey*, or, at the very least, imbued with a certain character and individuality, like *Millennium Falcon* in *Star Wars*. The spaceship is one focus for the bringing together of human and machine. Robots more obviously share human and machine characteristics. Lieutenant Commander Data, from *Star Trek: the Next Generation*, aspires to humanity; Superman is organic but has the strength and endurance of a machine, the 'man of steel'.

SPACESHIPS

In the first instance, a spaceship is simply a prop for moving characters around the SF universe, a car or a sailing ship translated into a futuristic idiom. Some spaceships in SF are nothing more than this; George Lucas's X-Wing fighters are figured in the battle scenes of *Star Wars*, as I have argued, as Second World War fighter planes relocated to outer space. At the same time, at a more suburban level of cultural symbolism these spaceships are higher-tech versions of the automobile, the same vehicle that figures so potently in Lucas's earlier movie *American Graffiti* (1973). That film is a cinematic reworking of Lucas's own small-town adolescence, and, in a more obviously coded way, so are the *Star Wars* films. Luke Skywalker (Luke S., a cipher for Lucas) can climb into his X-Wing fighter and 'drive' across the galaxy to park outside Yoda's jungle home, before 'driving' back to join his friends for the finale. It would not be correct to say that these sorts of spaceship are 'just' facilitators, because they are themselves fetishised, something that is evidenced by the fascination of fans with collecting models or getting hold of pseudo-technical specifications for these machines. But they do exist on a level where the metaphorical sense has not yet spilled over into Ship-as-Cyborg.

I should elaborate what I mean by this, because it is important to the argument I am making. Spaceships in SF come in two sorts: those that are 'just' machines, and those that are more than just machines, that can think for themselves, express personality and character, or that represent a combination of the human and the technological, such as McCaffrey's *Ship Who Sang* (1969). The *Millennium Falcon*, to take another example from *Star Wars*, is one of the former sort. It has more individuality than an X-Wing fighter, perhaps even a degree of 'personality' of its own, a cussed, ornery sort of personality, but this is only true in the way in which your old car may develop crotchets and quirks. It is a different sort of thing from *The Liberator*, the spaceship from the British TV series *Blake's-7* (1978–81), which possessed a computer mind of its own called 'Zen'. And yet, in one important respect, the *Millennium Falcon* is more than the sum of its parts. This is because the spaceships in an SF film are invested by us with a peculiar, almost human concentration of value, what Marxist theorists call 'reification'.

In the context of SF, this reification works most potently on the interconnected levels of representation of technology and the technologies of reproduction. Putting the matter crudely, people queuing up to see the latest *Star Wars* film are in large part waiting precisely to see the special effects. It is those effects which are so 'cool', which can dwarf the appeals of things like 'character' and 'plot'. It is possible to imagine a film where the plot and characterisation are utterly risible, but where the special effects are cool enough to mean that SF fans still take it to their hearts. Indeed, we really don't need to imagine this; we can think of many actual examples. Critics, and particularly film reviewers, sometimes complain about the dominance of special effects, but that is missing the point. The special effects in any given SF film, and, in a slightly different way, the technical marvels of more conventional written SF, *are* the point. The X-Wing fighters hurtling into the teeth of another space battle are characters in a very real sense. This is what reification means, and in critical terms one key effect is that, even when they are 'merely' hardware, or 'merely' facilitators, spaceships are still, in effect, cyborgs. They are both technology, like the blasters, and characters, like Han Solo or C3PO. This is why fans go to specialist shops and buy models of Tie-Fighters.

The richness of the situation, critically speaking, is that this reification of technology in SF cinema is actually a *self-reflexive* factor. The technology we fans admire so completely, the spaceships that we consider so cool and which are deployed on the screen before us in so exciting a fashion, are nothing more than the external trappings of the technology that we are really admiring, the technology of cinema itself. To say this is to connect with the theories of the postmodernist thinker Jean Baudrillard, who argues that the media imitation of 'reality' which he calls the 'simulacrum' has so replaced the real that it is all we have left. 'Reality' has been replaced by the *hyperreality* of our simulated world. In the realm of the Baudrillardian simulacrum, it is the technologies of simulation themselves that rule. This might appear to be a rather far-fetched claim, but it merits further consideration. Science as simulation is the reason why fictional science, or 'SF', is so much more exciting than real science; why *Star Wars* is more fun to watch than a real shuttle launch; why the adventures of the real-life space shuttle *Enterprise* were so much less enthralling than the adventures of the fictional *USS Enterprise*. The technologies of reproduction, particularly in the realm of special effects, are at a far more advanced stage of development than the actual technologies of space exploration. This also explains, I think, the contradictions experienced by those watching something like the *Challenger* disaster, in which a manned space shuttle exploded on ascent. On the one hand, this was something clearly appalling and tragic, something that moved many people to tears as it happened. But on another level, the live TV pictures bumped people from one mode of watching to another and gave a guilty undertow to the emotions. The *Challenger* launch was certainly the most memorable and, in a terrible way, the most exciting of all the shuttle launches; and shuttle launches are renowned for being dull, for always being delayed and postponed, and then for providing just another version of all the other shuttle launches we have seen when they finally happen. What *Challenger* did was suddenly to shift modes: from the 'real' mode of an actual launch to the 'SFX' mode of a film. In SF films spaceships explode all the time, and it is exciting. When *Challenger* exploded, the moment collapsed together our perceptions; that was one reason why, apart from being so terrible, it was so unsettling.

What spaceships do, then, in cinematic SF is focus our fascination with the medium itself. Spaceships are symbolic nova, but self-reflexive ones. To stay with *Star Wars* for a moment, there are two sorts of spaceships in these films: the very big and the ordinary-sized, which is to say car or truck-sized. The very big – the Imperial Cruisers, for instance, or the Death Star – are about technological *scale*; in effect, they are saying 'the technologies of cinema present us with very big things: sublime enormities on a screen much, much bigger than a TV screen'. The ordinary-sized are about issues of technological *speed*: X-Wings zooming along a trench in the side of the Death Star; the rapidity with which the technologies of cinema move things along; the excitements of speeding us through a narrative; and at root a fetishisation of the increasing speed of Western culture. Spaceships are the emblems of the technology that produces them, a technology of cultural reproduction rather than science.

Another way of working this metaphorical representation is through capaciousness, in other words through sheer size and scale. In works such as C. J. Cherryh's *Merchanters* series (beginning with the popular *Downbelow Station* in 1981), spaceships are more than facilitators; they are where people live. There is a branch of SF that insists on working within the constraints of Einsteinian physics, such that trips between stars have to take place at speeds less than that of light and therefore take decades or even centuries. In many examples of this SF the characters are compelled to live on their spaceships as worlds. The metaphor here seems straightforward enough: the spaceship is the world. In fact, as I have been arguing, the spaceship is actually 'the world of the text', which is to say 'the world of SF'. The spaceship in Brian Aldiss's *NonStop* (1958) is revealed to be a spaceship rather than a self-contained world only towards the end of the text; in other words, until the end we take the technological artefact to be organic.

Another famous spaceship, the *Discovery* from *2001: a Space Odyssey*, is part inanimate hardware, part thinking machine (the computer HAL). The disjunction between these two elements is emphasised by the voice of HAL, a softly spoken, breathy and warm voice that gains its sinister power in large part through how 'organic' it sounds, in stark contrast with both the inhumanly clean, antiseptic environment provided inside the ship and the scaffolding-and-sphere shape of the ship from the outside. When the computer goes mad, it does two things. On one level it crosses over from the conceptual territory of 'the machine' to that of the human; which is to say, where before it could play chess or engage in conversation, things we all accept that both humans and computers can do, after it does something we associate primarily with human beings: it becomes paranoid, kills, begs for its life and so on. But, on a different level, it gives us the sense that it is only making explicit something we have always half-wondered, half-feared of machines. It is the superstitious, even paranoid sense that machines all possess the potential to turn on us, to go mad, to express their character.

Paul McAuley's *Confluence* novels, *Child of the River* (1997), *Ancients of Days* (1998) and *Shrine of Stars* (1999), take this to a logical extreme. Confluence is an enormous world built long ago by human beings who raised up to sentience an enormous range of animals from all around the galaxy to inhabit it. It is a flat world with an artificial gravity operating across its surface that rocks back and forth to mimic sunrise and sunset. The makers of this enormous artefact, known as the Preservers, have long since fled the universe through a nearby black hole, but their creations continue to worship them as gods. The world of *Confluence* is one in which both machines and organic life interact in the fullest way imaginable. Billions of machines, from the enormous engines in the keel of the world to the myriad insect-like tiny machines that fly hither and thither through the sky, work constantly to maintain the world. The organic component of *Confluence* is similarly diverse, with a systematically encyclopedic range of animals given quasi-human consciousness and a range of approximations to human shape. Yama, the hero, is a point of connection: he is the only remaining example of the bloodline of the Builders, and as such he has telepathic control over the machines. He functions, in other words, as the point of connection between organic and technological. At the trilogy's conclusion, Confluence itself disintegrates and reveals itself to be a conglomeration of innumerable giant spaceships, 'the great ships which the Builders had joined together in the first act of the creation of the world' (McAuley, *Shrine of Stars* (1999): 312). These ships eventually fall apart again, 'a cloud of splinters shining in the light of the lonely star', on voyages to reoccupy the abandoned galaxy. *Confluence* becomes the seed from which organic life can grow throughout the cosmos.

ROBOTS

Czech author Karel Čapek's play *R.U.R.* (1921) is the place where the word 'robot' was coined (*robota* is Czech for 'drudgery' or 'servitude'), although Čapek's robots are not metallic but fleshy. This play is a deft little fable about exploitation, in which the robots eventually rise up against their oppressors. Robots were often invoked as ciphers for oppressed workers, sometimes in complex ways (for instance the robot Maria in Fritz Lang's film *Metropolis*, 1927). But as the trope of the robot became more embedded in SF, robots or androids came increasingly to be seen as a new race of beings. Perhaps the most famous robot storywriter was Isaac Asimov, who generally wrote the latter sort of story. With John Campbell, editor of *Astounding*, he formulated the 'three laws of robotics', which all robots in his imaginative universe must follow:

(1) a robot may not injure a human being or, through inaction, allow a human being to come to harm;

(2) a robot must obey the orders given it by human beings except where such orders would conflict with the First Law;

(3) a robot must protect its own existence as long as such protection does not conflict with the First or Second Law.

Asimov's 'robot' stories revolve largely around the narrative potentials inherent in exploring or contravening these rules. But the main effect of his 'three laws of robotics' is to foreground the *ethical* in the delineation of the machine. Asimov's robots are supremely ethical machines, governed in the first instance by a desire to preserve and aid human life. Because the ethical imperative is so central to their conception, Asimov's robots are necessarily attractive and humanised creations. In terms of the representation of difference, they embody a mapping on to a technological framework of more everyday social differences. As Edward James puts it, 'it is difficult not to see Asimov's *Caves of Steel* (1953), with its robots who take ordinary people's jobs and even "pass for human", as a comment upon relations between whites and blacks in America' (James 1994: 89).

The sinister potential of 'the robot' has provided many SF texts with their organising structure. In Michael Crichton's *Westworld* (1973) fun-seekers can spend a holiday in a re-creation of the wild west or of medieval England or ancient Rome, peopled by robots. In Westworld itself, holidaymakers are given guns with sensors that distinguish human from machine, so they can shoot the robots to their heart's content but can't accidentally injure one another. Things, of course, go wrong, something signified by the fact that the robot gunslinger Yul Brynner starts killing people. Apparently the guns, and the robots themselves, no longer distinguish human from machine. A cameo at the end of the film emphasises this: the protagonist, having escaped death at the hands of the malfunctioning gunslinger robot, finds a woman chained in a dungeon begging for water. He gives her a drink and thereby fuses her circuits; she had been a robot all along. It is impossible to tell human and machine apart.

In Ridley Scott's *Alien* (1979), crewmember Ash, played by Ian Holm, is an android with sinister intentions that include murdering his crewmates if necessary. But the confusion between human and machine goes beyond the fact that his crewmates, and the audience, don't realise that he is a machine until late in the film. More than this is the fact that, unlike the 'dry' technology of electrical circuitry that lies beneath Yul Brynner's artificial skin in *Westworld*, Ash is constructed out of an organic-looking 'wet' technology, so that when injured he spurts out what we take to be hydraulic fluid, and his viscera are a series of disconcerting slippery tubes and conduits. In Bukatman's words, 'the android, Ash, is both organic and inorganic as well, and "his" destruction is marked by the gushing forth of the milky fluids that constitute "his" "blood" ' (Bukatman 1993: 266). There is something inherently unsettling about this superimposition of organic and machine, something that finds its most efficient expression in the robot for the obvious reason that robots are designed precisely to look like human beings. Ridley Scott's cinematic version of Dick's *Do Androids Dream of Electric Sheep?*, the film *Blade Runner* (1982), presents its robots, or 'replicants', as fleshly machines that breathe, bleed and eventually die precisely in order to be able to work through questions relating to how we define 'human'. Scott's replicants look human and are in fact represented as childlike. Designed with only four years of life, they have, despite their adult bodies and intelligence, many of the unformed attitudes of children. This is in spite of the fact that they are ruthless killers who murder a number of people in the course of the film. When the chief replicant, Roy, steps into the apartment of the human Sebastian, which is full of life-size mechanised automata, he speaks like an excited child: 'Gosh – you've got a lot of great toys here!' Confronting the fact that all their fellow replicants have died, the female robot Pris responds not with grief but instead with a petulant line delivered with the intonation of a 2-year-old: 'but then we're stupid and we'll die!' It is this combination of human, childlike innocence and ingenuousness with a machine-like strength and ruthlessness that provides the replicants with their uncanny metaphoric potency.

In other words, the robot is that place in an SF text where technological and human are most directly blended. The robot is the dramatisation of the alterity of the machine, the paranoid sense of the inorganic come to life. That it works this way, rather than just clothing the human in mechanical dress, is indicated by a few key examples. When Douglas Adams fictionalises a robot with what his 'Sirius Cybernetics Corporation' calls 'Genuine People Personalities' or 'GPPs', the result can only be expressed in a comic mode. Adams' radio series *The Hitchhiker's Guide to the Galaxy* (1978–1980) is a deft and often hilarious satire on many SF tropes. But it is Marvin, the enormously intelligent but chronically depressed android whose metallic clanking along with the hydraulic puffs and gasps that accompany his movement suggest that he is more robot than android, who remains one of the most enduring creations of the series. Marvin combines the attributes of the most advanced of machine intelligences with the pathological character traits of a particularly flawed human being. He has, as he repeatedly insists, 'a brain the size of a planet'; he is so intelligent that he can read human consciousness; and he is so durable that he can, and in one episode does, live from now until the literal end of the universe, however many billennia that represents. But at the same time he is so continually depressed and miserable that it is a chore having to be around him; he hates everything, including himself, and he is able literally to bore some security guards to death merely by telling them his miserable life story. The joke, that robots given 'Genuine People Personalities' might also develop Genuine People Personality Disorders, might seem a thin one to spin out over twelve episodes, but the glory of Marvin's characterisation is that he pursues the expression of his depression with machine-like rigour, so that he not only adds human characteristics to his machineness, he also adds machine characteristics to his human traits. He is a potently thorough blending of machine and man. A less effective example of the same trope is the animated film *Robots* (2005), which imagines a wholly mechanical world filled with robotic characters, yet strives to achieve comic effect by blending organic elements (these robots seem continually to be farting, for instance).

By now the terms of the debate have shifted from technology as such and on to that creature I touched on first in Chapter 3 and again earlier in the present chapter: the cyborg. We have already encountered Donna Harraway's influential essay on the cyborg, a quasi-feminist manifesto aimed at reclaiming the positive aspects of cyborg existence. But Harraway is quite forthright about the 'perversity' of her positive feminist reappropriation of this SF icon. The reason for this is that, Marvin aside, most SF cyborgs have used their unsettling connotations to represent evil. A figure such as Arnold Schwarzenegger's embodiment of a killer cyborg sets himself absolutely against humanity. As Jonathan

Goldberg points out: '*The Terminator* embodies a "new order of intelligence" that is resolutely anti-human and anti-reproductive.' His task in the movie 'is nothing less than a mission to ensure the end of the human race' (Gray *et al.* 1995: 243). Even here, though, the representation of difference in the shape of the cyborg has its interesting potentials. One populist manifestation of the cyborg, the Borg from the *Star Trek* franchises, actually forces the issue of alterity in a radical manner, taking the revaluation of all values to its logical extreme. Bringing together organic and machine in a stylishly designed package, the Borg represent the most extreme foe the Federation has yet encountered. The Borg appeared in certain *Next Generation* episodes, most notably 'The Best of Both Worlds', and were so popular with fans that they have been often resurrected. It is interesting to consider exactly what is so appealing to *Trek* fans about the Borg.

One of the points of audience connection with the Borg, it seems to me, is precisely their old-fashionedness. Their technology, although being, as many characters repeatedly assert, greatly superior to anything the Federation has, *looks* very old. The styling of the Borg is retrograde; all those tubes and whirring devices, and the tiny little revolving satellite dishes on the top of their heads, are old fashioned, like something out of the 1950s; you won't find any satellite dishes whirring on the sleekly futuristic *Enterprise*. Moreover, because they are 'old fashioned', the Borg enact the fertile contradiction at the heart of SF, the collision of future and past, of prophetic and nostalgic modes. There is another way in which we, as audience, register this retro difference: the Borg are 'black and white', not just in the sense that their costumes are black leather and plastic and their skin pale, but in a more literal sense. In 'The Best of Both Worlds' Captain Picard is captured by the Borg and turned into a drone; in one scene the Captain is on a Borg operating table, and a probe of some kind is inserted into the side of his head, causing the colour literally to drain from his face. It is as if the Borg belong to a realm of black-and-white film, and this contrast is emphasised by the first team to beam over to the Borg ship from the *Enterprise*: the colourful uniforms of the members of this team (actually primary colours: Shelby in red, Crusher in blue, Worf and Data in yellow) seem garish in the colour-restricted environment of the Borg ship. We might argue that the Borg point to a cinematic aesthetic, that they are emblematic representatives of clunky black-and-white cinema, whilst the *Enterprise* belongs in the world of colour TV.

The Borg 'collective', in which all individuality is utterly squashed and everyone works for the good of the whole, appears at first sight as a rather crude satire on communism, pitted against the 'American' individuality of the *Enterprise* crew. But the Borg have a vitality (paradoxically) that supersedes any one narrowly allegorical reading of their significance. Taylor Harrison, for example, sees the Borg as representative of death, or, more specifically, he has read the Borg episodes of *Next Generation* as a coded representation of the AIDS epidemic (Harrison 1996: 257). The *Next Generation* film *First Contact*, as another example, sees the Borg reimagined not as communists but as vampires. And more potent, I think, is the way 'The Best of Both Worlds' expresses one aspect of the vigorous American Zeitgeist, alien abduction. Communism and the evil Russian Empire are old news, the dustbin of history. Alien abduction, on the other hand, is bang up to date, one of the key narratives of the contemporary US. The scene where Picard, who has been, quite literally, abducted by aliens, is laid out on some sort of operating table and has probes inserted into his head is the most explicit reference to this cultural narrative. But over and above these partial interpretations of the Borg is the fact that they remain one of the most thorough and effective attempts by SF writers working in a popular idiom to represent an alterity that is genuinely other.

The emphasis upon alterity expands our sense of the radical otherness of the Borg in this context. The Borg as they originally appear represent everything the Federation is not, focusing our attention on the way their mode of being is literally beyond our ability to comprehend. This is the true nature of 'otherness'; an alien would be not 'basically like you or me but with pointy ears' (like Spock), but instead radically and totally unlike you or me or anything we can conceive. So, where Federation, which is to say human, culture is based on individuality, on what Picard proudly insists in the face of the Borg ship is 'freedom and self-determination', the Borg culture is not. Where human culture is hierarchical, so that Picard is in charge, with everybody else on the *Enterprise* ranked in some set position beneath him, there are no ranks or hierarchies on the Borg ship. The Federation is a *centred* civilisation; which is to say, it is literally centred on what the series refers to several times as 'sector zero zero one', or Earth, and also metaphorically centred on certain core values, the beliefs and ideologies at the centre of human existence which give purpose and meaning to our lives. The Borg have no centre; they have no purpose or meaning and don't need them. The postmodern theory of contemporary French thinkers Gilles Deleuze and Felix Guattari distinguishes between, on the one hand, the 'arboreal' or 'tree-like' logics of more traditional cultures, which like a tree function in one up–down direction, are hierarchical and restricted, and, on the other hand, the 'rhizomatic' or 'root-like' logics of postmodernism, which, like a system of roots under the soil, make all manner of interesting connections in all sorts of directions and dimensions. According to this postmodern perspective, the Borg are rhizomatic, decentred and associative; the Federation, on the other hand, is arboreal, centred and structured. The Borg do without notions of 'individuality', of 'centre' or 'structure', of 'purpose' or 'meaning'; they have, as Worf gruffly points out, 'neither Honor nor Courage' and have no need of them. They do not value any of the things that we value; they dismiss, in turn, 'strength', 'freedom', 'self-determination' and 'death'. In fact, they seem to do without the very notion of 'value'. This, I suggest, is a bold stab by the *Star Trek* scriptwriters at presenting something *radically* other, something with which the human-centred Federation really has nothing in common. To emphasise the point, the boldness here is in *doing the representing*. There are SF texts, such as *2001* or *Contact*, which are prepared to posit a radical otherness in their aliens, but they also duck out of the challenge of representing it. Not so *Star Trek*. It is this sense of utter difference, of a discontinuity which cannot be breached, that underlies what have always struck me as some of the most chillingly effective lines in TV science fiction. When the captured Picard is taken aboard the Borg ship and argues with the disembodied voice of the Borg, he seems, literally, to be speaking to the whole ship. Picard states the key values of the Federation, the key values, arguably, of any 'life form', and in each case the Borg simply negate them, ultimately negating life itself. They do this not in the sense that they 'value' destroying life or killing, as a warrior race might, but rather in the utterly other sense that neither life nor death is of any importance.

PICARD: I will resist you with my last ounce of strength.

THE BORG: Strength is irrelevant. Resistance is futile fi Your culture will adapt to service ours.

PICARD: Impossible! My culture is based on freedom and self-determination.

THE BORG: Freedom is irrelevant. Self-determination is irrelevant. You must comply.

PICARD: We would rather die.

THE BORG: Death is irrelevant.

The power of this exchange resides less in the way the Borg assert something, for instance that they are 'stronger' than the Federation and can force complicity; after all, as they say, 'strength is irrelevant'. More powerful is their extraordinary statement of values, or rather of anti-values. The construction that such-and-such 'is irrelevant' does not even engage in a dialectic with the thing in question, because to do that would be to suggest that because the Borg are prepared to engage with it, the thing in question has some value. But they are utterly dismissive. The Borg do not say 'your strength is insufficient', which, by implication, would imply 'we value our superior strength'. Instead they say 'strength', with the implication of all strength, yours, ours, 'is irrelevant'. It does not figure. Similarly, and most radically, they do not even value life, the being that is most basic to any humanist conception of existence. It is impossible for us to enter imaginatively into the world of the Borg because certain key values we hold, values like individuality, life/death and so on, are too centrally part of us, whereas for the Borg they are neither good nor bad but simply irrelevant.

CYBERSPACE

'Cyberspace' is a term in increasing currency today. It refers to the notional space of the internet and virtual reality, to the computer-generated environments into which human beings can enter through a computer or a virtual-reality suit. In reality this 'space' is fairly limited, but many science-fiction texts posit a time when cyberspace is an exciting and dynamic realm of possibilities. Its cognate SF sub-genre is cyberpunk.

Cyberpunk is that contemporary mode of SF most implicated with technology. Indeed, Samuel Delany sees all cyberpunk as necessarily pro-technology, as a way of seeing and representing the world that prioritises the technological over the psychological, with obvious implications for the kind of fiction written under its aegis.

> Cyberpunk is pro-tech, it is apsychological ... Cyberspace exists merely as a technological consensus. Without that technology it could not exist, be entered, or function. It's much closer to Popper's notion of 'World-3' (the world of texts and data that interweaves and stabilizes the world of human beings) or Chardin's 'Noosphere' (the circle of abstract knowledges presumed to be generated by and encircling the biosphere) than it is to anything internal or psychological.
>
> (Delany 1994: 176)

George Slusser says something similar when he classifies SF as 'an infosphere', with cyberpunk as the 'informational conscience' of the genre.

> In the cyberpunk world, to write SF is to make physical, even visceral contact with the mechanical and biological extensions of our personal infosphere (cyborgs, grafts, prostheses, clones), and beyond that with the image surrogates themselves (simulations, 'constructs', holograms) that now crowd and share our traditional fictional living space.
>
> (Slusser and Shippey 1992: 3)

Slusser's point has something to do with the materiality of SF, which I discussed earlier, the way SF provides concrete, material externalisations for metaphors of alterity. But he is also suggesting a close enough affinity between SF as literature and the reality of existence in the West today under the cultural logic critics call 'postmodernism'. We encountered this earlier, in Baudrillard's argument that contemporary culture involves us in a supersession of reality by simulacra. The extent to which postmodernism as a cultural logic depends upon today's advanced technology is rarely stressed by critics of that phenomenon; but it is precisely that technology, and most especially today's technologies of mass reproduction, the TV, the computer, that determines and defines postmodernity. And it is the coming together of TV and computer that informs cyberspace, one of the most potent of the technological metaphors to come out of SF.

Its vogue may now (2005) have run its course, but for much of the 1980s and 1990s 'cyberpunk' was the dominant mode of popular SF. Ridley Scott's film *Blade Runner* (1982) and William Gibson's novel *Neuromancer* (1984) were followed by many imitators. Some of these were derivative, but many achieved genuine artistic success. Masamune Shirow created a detailed and beautiful visual artefact leavened with philosophical pretension in the futuristic cyborg spy-thriller *Ghost in the Shell* (the original Japanese title, *Kokaku Kidotai*, means literally 'Mobile Armoured Riot Police'). Neal Stephenson's novel *Snow Crash* (1993) adds a humorous satirical perspective to the conventions of the form. By the end of the century the premise of 'cyberspace' as a viable alternate simulacrum to actual reality was common enough currency to support a blockbuster movie, *The Matrix* (directed by the Wachowski Brothers, 1999).

CASE STUDY: WILLIAM GIBSON, *NEUROMANCER* (1984)

Far from being a celebration of technology, William Gibson's *Neuromancer* (1984) articulates a distinctively double-edged attitude to the machine. On the one hand, this is a text that delights in the ingenious and fascinating toys its imaginative universe produces, although, given the spy/crime genre Gibson is working in, this delight is expressed chiefly in terms of the damage the technology can do: how effective the weaponry is, how deadly Molly's implants are, and so on. But simultaneously the technology in this imaginative universe is almost always threatening, alienating, a negative quantity. The fact that his technology is always what antique dealers call 'distressed', that is to say the creation of a sense of rough edges, broken components and all-round decay, is one of the most noteworthy features of the Gibsonian style. In part his novel reads like an aesthetic attack on the notion of technology itself, a sort of textual bashing of the stuff of the narrative. One of the things Gibson does best is create the same sense of ambient technological paranoia that Philip K Dick achieves so perfectly, and Dick's *Ubik* serves as a sort of intertextual template here. The Gibsonian universe presents a world where humans battle to survive in an urban jungle, but the most dangerous predators in this jungle are the machines. At times Gibson eerily captures exactly the unease with which we can regard the familiar technological props of our own lives, such as phones, TVs and microwaves – the way in which they seem almost to have a life of their own. His character Case's first encounter with Wintermute, the Artificial Intelligence or 'AI' that is arguably the novel's chief protagonist, manages this tone of technology-paranoid sensibility perfectly.

This notion of haunting is behind the ethical conceit of the novel as well; in so far as the novel explores an ethical grey area, it has to do with whether Wintermute 'should' or 'shouldn't' be allowed to upgrade itself, to become more perfect and complete, and possibly fully sentient. Wintermute itself sees this as an evolutionary matter: 'You're always building models. Stone circles. Cathedrals. Pipe Organs. Adding machines. I got no idea why I'm here, you know that? But if the run goes off tonight, you'll have finally managed the real thing' (p. 204). Other characters in the novel see it in terms of a pact with the Devil. As Wintermute says: 'The French girl, she said you were selling out the species. Demon, she said I was ... it doesn't much matter' (p. 205). The French girl, Michele, conceives the terms of the exchange as a throwback negotiation, this being the first place where the resonances of the 'neuromancer' (necromancer) title start to bite:

'You are worse than a fool,' Michele said, getting to her feet, the pistol in her hand. 'You have no care for your species. For thousands of years men dreamed of pacts with demons. Only now are such things possible. And what would you be paid with?'

(Gibson, *Neuromancer* (1984): 193)

This is the atavistic scheme underlying the apparently forward-looking ethos of the novel; and it is at this point that technology and magic become, as is often the case in SF, only a matter of perspective. In this sense, *Neuromancer* is as nostalgic, as backward-looking an American SF text as any.

Cyberpunk, more thoroughly and systematically than any other SF novum, is built around the process of metaphor. Cyberspace itself is not a real space but a notional space, a metaphorical space. In Gibson's novel it is described in literal, visual terms, although the narrative repeats several times that it is not a literal or visual space, but rather a 'nonspace' (p. 81). Gibson conceded that this imaginary environment was based not on any personal experience of the world of computing, since he had no such experience, but upon the video games his children played. Accordingly, description in *Neuromancer* often adopts an almost facile, video-gamelike quality:

> Faint kaleidoscopic angles centred in to a silver-black point. Case watched childhood symbols of evil and bad luck tumble out along translucent planes: swastikas, skulls and crossbones, dice flashing snake eyes ... [At the core there was] a shark thing, gleaming like obsidian ... 'That's the sting,' the construct said.
>
> (Gibson, *Neuromancer* (1984): 216)

On this level, there is an almost small-minded literalism about Gibson's cyberspace: a programme designed to protect information appears as a shark, scattering signs of ill omen around it. But what this space does is to articulate the action of metaphor; this defensive programme will not only 'bite' you *like* an angry shark, it actually *is* an angry shark, at least in the world it inhabits. The same holds for 'ICE', a substance that gets its name simply enough from its acronym: it is a software that protects against intrusion, and so is called 'Intrusion Countermeasure Electronics'. But when we encounter 'ICE' in the world of Gibson's cyberspace, it functions at both levels at once, as metaphor and as literalism:

> Ice patterns formed and reformed on the screen as he probed for gaps, skirted the most obvious traps, and mapped the route he'd take through Sense/Net's ice. It was good ice. Wonderful ice. Its patterns burned there while he lay with his arm under Molly's shoulders.
>
> (Gibson, *Neuromancer* (1984): 76)

A great deal of Gibson's prose mediates in this fashion between the literal and the metaphorical; and the overall effect for the novel as a whole is to create a finely balanced textual construct, something that could go either way, capable of being read either as a gritty-realist account of actual existence or as a symbolist text, almost an allegory, of the episte-mological hunt, the search for knowledge and meaning.

This double perspective feeds through into all sorts of aspects of Gibson's descriptive world. Take this description of cyberspace:

> He punched himself through and found an infinite blue space ranged with color-coded spheres strung on a tight grid of pale blue neon. In the nonspace of the matrix, the interior of a given data construct pos-sessed unlimited subjective dimension; a child's toy calculator, accessed through Case's Sendai, would have presented limitless gulfs of nothingness hung with a few basic commands.
>
> (Gibson, *Neuromancer* (1984): 81)

What is oxymoronic about this piece of description at a localised level – which is to say, how can this space be both a 'tight grid' and an 'infinite blue space', how can 'neon' be 'pale' and so on – actually only figures the larger sense in which Gibson deliberately unsettles our textual expecta-tions in order to convey the paradoxical status of this space. The effect of this, in the end, is almost spiritual, which is one reason why the Japanese figuring of this tale, both the technology used in it and the actual setting for many scenes, is so appropriate. Underlying this streetwise, distressed-tech narrative is an almost Zen artistic vision, where infinity can be glimpsed in the simplest thing, where a 'child's toy calculator' can pre-sent 'limitless gulfs of nothingness' to the trained perception. The effect of *this* is presumably to elevate cyberspace into a near-magical realm, a realm where humanity is freed from the constraints of the flesh, what the novel calls 'meat', so that we can soar like the angels. Cyberspace becomes an almost religious experience. Compare, for instance, the way the book's first sex scene describes orgasm: Case and Molly have sex 'until they both had come, his orgasm flaring blue in timeless space, a vastness like the matrix, where the faces were shredded and blown away down hurricane corridors' (p. 45). It is as if orgasm, briefly, reaches the peak where cyberspace is all the time, that, by implication, cyberspace is the ultimate intensity of physical experience.

This metaphorical theme inhabits all the levels of the text. It is there in the prose style, the building blocks of the novel, and it is also there on the level of the novel's conception, the metaphor that is cyberspace. But it goes deeper than that. Of the characters who appear in the novel, some are 'real' characters, some are 'constructs', or more accurately metaphors standing in for characters. But how easy is it to distinguish between these different sorts of character? Case's erstwhile colleague Dix is an interesting example. Case resurrects this character from death, something articulated in the flat matrix of the novel without biblical or religious overtones, such that even the tag 'Lazarus of cyberspace' (p. 98) functions as a blank reference. Dix comes back as a 'construct'. To begin with he is 'directionless' in more senses than one:

> [Case] coughed. 'Dix? McCoy? That you man?' His throat was tight.
>
> 'Hey bro,' said a directionless voice.
>
> 'It's Case, man. Remember?'
>
> 'Miami, joeboy, quick study.'
>
> 'What's the last thing you remember before I spoke to you, Dix?'
>
> 'Nothin'.'
>
> 'Hang on.' He disconnected the construct. The presence was gone.
>
> He reconnected it. 'Dix? Who am I?'
>
> 'You got me hung, Jack. Who the fuck are you?'
>
> 'Case – your buddy. Partner. What's happening man?'
>
> 'Good question.'
>
> 'Remember being here, a second ago?'
>
> 'No.'
>
> 'Know how a ROM personality matrix works?'
>
> 'Sure, bro, it's a firmware construct.'
>
> …
>
> 'Okay, Dix. You are a ROM construct. Got me?'
>
> 'If you say so,' said the construct. 'Who are you?'
>
> (Gibson, *Neuromancer* (1984): 99)

This is only a metaphorical person, a series of computer algorithms that can mimic the particular speech habits of the dead individual: 'what's happening man?', 'who the fuck are you?' But it cannot achieve any sense of self-identity, because it isn't 'real'. This makes Dix totally predictable, which is one key difference between himself and 'real' people.

Later Wintermute says, 'you guys … you're a pain. The Flatline here, if you were all like him, it would be real simple. He's a construct, just a bunch of ROM, so he always does what I expect him to. My projections said there wasn't much chance of Molly wandering in on Ashpool's big exit scene, give you one example' (p. 245).

But one of the things that happens as the book proceeds is a sense of Gibson fleshing out the famous experiment devised by Alan Turing, the pioneer of computing practice and theory in the 1940s and 1950s, to test whether a machine can ever achieve 'consciousness'. The Turing Test postulates a closed space, in which there might be a human being or a computer. Turing wondered how many questions it would take a human experimenter before he or she could determine who or what was in the box. In the early days of computing it was relatively easy to detect a computer's responses; as computing becomes increasingly sophisticated, so it gets harder. In Gibson's novel, Dix is a dramatisation of the Turing Test. He seems to do everything a consciousness does; and by this I mean more than that he answers back, and laughs, and thinks: I mean that he desires in a way a machine cannot desire – he desires to die. 'Hey asshole,' he says to Wintermute, '… what about me? what about my payoff?' Case asks him what his payoff from Wintermute is to be. 'I want to be erased,' the construct said. 'I told you that, remember?' (p. 246). Dix is 'bothered' by his limbo status; the construct is self-aware and unhappy with its self-awareness:

> 'How you doing, Dixie?'
>   'I'm dead, Case …'
>   'How's it feel?'
>   'It doesn't.'
>   'Bother you?'
>   'What bothers me is, nothin' does.'
>
> (Gibson, *Neuromancer* (1984): 130)

Dix is only one of the characters who are presented to us as a way of problematising our accepted, traditional notions of character. Armitage, unlike Dix, appears to be flesh and blood, as real as any human being. But, as the novel progresses, the other characters start to have their doubts: 'that guy doesn't have any life going, in private

... Sits and stares at the wall man' (p. 117). We slowly realise that 'Armitage' is a sort of flesh construct, a ROM personality built around the recovered fragments of a 'real' personality called Corto, who was nearly killed on the 'Screaming Fist' military raid. Corto eventually breaks through Armitage, but Corto is insane where Armitage was rational; Corto sets off and kills himself where Armitage displayed habits of self-preservation. In other words, Corto is less 'real' a character than the artificial 'Armitage'. The novel is full of 'real' characters who act like zombies, like the prostitutes in the Freeside brothel who operate with a neural cut-out so that they don't have to experience the things they do. On the other hand, one of the most vivid 'characters' in the novel is Wintermute himself, who is not 'real', at least until the end. The net effect of all this is to create a situation where 'real' and 'construct' start to blur. Immediately after Wintermute complains to Case that constructs like Dix are predictable and human beings are not, Case asks why the old man Ashpool committed suicide. Wintermute's reply starts with a standard disavowal that he doesn't know because humans are simply unpredictable; but he goes on to admit not only that he knows the reason for the suicide, but that he prompted it, in an indirect way. In other words, Ashpool was as 'predictable' as any AI:

> 'Why does anybody kill himself?' The figure shrugged. 'I guess I know, if anybody does, but it would take me twelve hours to explain the various factors in his history and how they interrelate ... 3Jane figured a way to fiddle the program that controlled his cryogenic system ... so basically *she* killed him ... Well, actually, I guess I did give 3Jane the odd hint ...'
>
> (Gibson, *Neuromancer* (1984): 245)

Wintermute frequently comes over in this novel as – a significant pun – virtually omniscient, god-like. This could be an instance of the SF text that plays with secular versions of religious notions, a novel without a god that invents one, a computer one, as it goes on. Or perhaps we should follow the French girl's analysis and think in terms less of God and more of demons. At one point inside Wintermute, Case gets to the root of the issue of identity that I have been interrogating here,

the suggestion that even our own 'identity', that sense of ourselves that
we prize so dearly, may only be a 'metaphor' too:

> 'Can you read my mind, Finn?' He grimaced. 'Wintermute, I mean.'
>
> 'Minds aren't *read*. See, you've still got the paradigms print gave
> you, and you're barely print-literate. I can access your memory, but
> that's not the same as your mind.'
>
> (Gibson, Neuromancer (1984): 204)

Case and Wintermute are here trading different metaphors of consciousness. Case falls back on the idea that consciousness is like a book,
like the book we are reading perhaps; this is a suitably self-reflexive
notion, because, of course, literally, Case's consciousness is like a book,
in fact it *is* a book. Wintermute, on the other hand, insists that consciousness is like a computer program. This debate is essentially a
philosophical debate, something *Neuromancer* is full of. For instance,
Case, trapped inside Wintermute's cyberspace imitation of reality, is
curious as to whether the computer simulation continues out of the
window to include things he can't see. Wintermute refers to the
famous philosophical question associated with English eighteenth-
century thinker George Berkeley, who wondered whether a tree that
falls in the forest where nobody sees it makes a sound. Case looks out
the virtual window and asks, 'what's out there? New York? Or does it
just stop?' 'Well,' Wintermute replies, 'it's like that tree, you know?
Falls in the woods, but maybe there's nobody to hear it' (p. 203). This
novel inhabits the philosophical space that argues over the question of
'consciousness', something philosophers have been arguing over for
thousands of years.

Neuromancer is a wonderfully tightly controlled work of art. The symbolic novum of the novel reflects lucidly back on our experience of living in the world, whilst allowing the startling and poetic encounter
with otherness that is the strength of the science-fictional mode. Scott
Bukatman thinks that cyberpunk 'remains the most sustained manifestation' of what he calls 'terminal identity', the computer-mediated end
of old models of subjectivity, in contemporary culture; and he regards
Gibson as 'indisputably the finest of the cyberpunk writers' because 'he
is the most poetic, and the most physical – the most erotic ... in the cli-

mactic cyberspatial transcendence at the end of *Neuromancer*, Case's mouth fills with "the aching taste of blue" – perhaps the taste of the machine, the taste of technology' (Bukatman 1993: 328–9). Science fiction is still the best way to experience that distinctive, strange and impossible taste.

6

CONCLUSION

I want to conclude not by simply summing up what I have said in the previous chapters, but by trying to tie together some of the threads of my argument by picking up the argument advanced in the last chapter. The question is whether science fiction is a *metaphorical* discourse or not, whether, in fact, everything I have previously said can be boiled down to this notion of the genre as 'other-imagery', or metaphor. This is a large question, and it connects to the problem of the status of metaphor itself, which is much larger.

To start with a single, apparently straightforward instance. The film *The Matrix* (directed by the Wachowski brothers, 1999) is premised on the idea that day-to-day life is a virtual-reality prison constructed by machine-intelligences. It does not mean this statement literally. It means it metaphorically; we are not *really* living in a virtual-reality prison, although this is a useful *metaphorical* way of talking about contemporary life. Is this what distinguishes this particular SF text, and by extension all SF texts, from 'realist' texts? The TV series *Sopranos*, say, presents life as a gangster literally; *The Matrix* presents life as computer-generated medium metaphorically. Does that touch on a basic truth about SF? What implications might that statement have?

METAPHOR

It seems at first that the question is straightforward. For Aristotle in his *Rhetoric* the point of metaphor is its otherness: one noun is substituted for another noun, the substitution being, in Greek, *allotropos* or 'alien'. 'Achilles is a man' is not a metaphor, but 'Achilles is a lion' is. We understand that Achilles is not literally a lion, but rather that he is 'like' a lion in some way. Metaphorically comparing Achilles to the lion means translating the noun 'Achilles' into the quite different noun 'lion'. The difference is the whole point of the exercise: a metaphor allows us to see a familiar thing in a new light. This is what is at stake in metaphor: Juliet is the sun; Eric Clapton is God; day-to-day life is a virtual-reality prison constructed by machine-intelligences. If Shakespeare had said 'Juliet is *like* the sun', he would, strictly, have been employing simile rather than metaphor; but the effect, though weakened, would have been pretty much the same.

This surely sounds very like science fiction. In SF we have a world made strange in some creative, useful way. Darko Suvin's novum, as I argued in the first chapter, is crucial to his definition of the genre: a novum is the point of difference between a 'realist' text and a SF text. We might say, simplifying somewhat, that Suvin's novum defines SF as a metaphorical mode of literature.

Certainly, many critics are quite comfortable with the general definition of SF as 'metaphoric fiction'. According to this model, 'realist' or 'mimetic' fiction attempts to represent the world as it 'actually' is, where metaphoric fiction invokes a translation of this actual world through one or other algorithm of difference. Peter Stockwell spends several chapters of his *Poetics of Science Fiction* (2000) embroidering his statement that 'the whole field of metaphor is centrally important for science fiction poetics' (Stockwell 2000: 169), deploying as he does so a large number of complicated technical terms. Metaphor is often invoked as the strategy of the SF text, as when Scott Bukatman says of Barry Malzberg's experimental novel *Galaxies*: 'the drama of the starship being dragged into the maw of a black hole provides a metaphor for the breakdown of narrative causality and sequence' (Bukatman 1993: 174; he adds 'but the reverse is also true').

Suvin himself has explored the question in his essay 'SF as Metaphor, Parable and Chronotope' in *Positions and Presuppositions in Science Fiction*

(1988). There he argues that to have value a SF tale needs not only metaphoricity but also 'coherence and richness'. He reads Cordwainer Smith's story 'The Lady Who Sailed *The Soul*' in terms of its complex of metaphorical levels. But detailed and compelling though his criticism is, it does not dispose of all the problems of seeing SF as metaphor. One such problem is that the one-to-one mapping implied by metaphor at its most basic level (Suvin calls it 'micro-metaphor') tends towards the reductive: 'I do not see how any micro-metaphor, however drawn out,' he notes, 'could accommodate more than two agents (that is, more than one action)' (Suvin 1988: 202). If SF is a metaphor, then the resonance of its texts will be limited. 'Achilles is a lion' means that Achilles is strong, beautiful, predatory, ruthless, but it cannot mean that Achilles is weak, or eloquent, or wearing plaid, or many other things. To say '*Dune* is a metaphor' or '*Solaris* is a metaphor' is to shrink those texts to a limited field of signification.

Suvin addresses this problem by insisting that 'any metaphor that goes beyond one sentence begins to organize a narrative argument' and that SF 'is generally acknowledged to be somewhere in between metaphor and story – the parable' (Suvin 1988: 199). But a parable, such as the biblical parable of the talents, is similarly reducible to one interpretation; it does not generate the imaginative surplus (the qualia, the density of lived experience) of textual depth because the reading of the parable is always steered towards one interpretation. Metaphor on this level (Suvin calls it 'model or macro-metaphor') is surely as limiting as micro-metaphor.

Another problem is identified by Patrick Parrinder in his intelligent analysis of Suvin's work. Most theorists argue that metaphors absolutely permeate all our language and discourse. To base a theory of SF on metaphor blurs distinctions between SF and other forms of literature. After all, some might say that Dickens' novels are, in their way, just as metaphoric as Cordwainer Smith. Suvin's model, says Parrinder,

> quickly leads to a *reductio ad absurdum*, since most modern linguistic theorists would maintain that metaphor is ubiquitous to and constitutive of language itself ... the further we follow Suvin in this, the more inescapable seems his tacit abandonment of the idea of science fiction as a special kind of narrative exhibiting cognitive estrangement

… In the later writings, in which Suvin considers metaphor as a fundamental aesthetic and cognitive gesture, all aesthetic manifestations in the medium of language seem to entail a cognitive element. Claiming that SF merely exemplifies far more widespread aspects of the process of thinking and making analogies, Suvin's own analogical mode of thought expands his 'poetics of SF' well past breaking point.

(Parrinder 2000: 46)

The point is that metaphor is everywhere. When we say 'the sun rises' we employ a metaphor, since we know of course that the sun doesn't literally rise; if somebody says 'isn't it hot today?' and we reply 'yes, boiling hot', we are speaking metaphorically. If I say 'These shoes are killing me' or 'I'm ecstatic' or 'he's a real beast', I speak metaphorically. Nietzsche noticed this feature of discourse, the way our speech is stitched together from 'dead metaphors', in 1873: 'what then is truth? A mobile army of metaphors … truths are illusions about which one has forgotten that this is what they are; metaphors which are worn out and without sensual power' (Nietzsche (1873): 46–7).

French philosopher Jacques Derrida's classic 1971 essay 'White Mythologies' (in *Margins of Philosophy*) expands Nietzsche's insight. Karl Simms summarises the essay:

Derrida's claim is that all philosophising is infected with a blindness to the metaphoricity of the language in which it is expressed. Metaphor is more than a special effect within language; it is the very essence of language. Even a philosophy of metaphor is itself inescapably metaphorical, so that metaphor cannot be adequately defined outside its own system. Metaphor thus runs out of control through language and through philosophy, the whole of philosophical discourse being an edifice built entirely upon itself without grounding in reality, and sustaining itself by an active forgetting of this fact.

(Simms 2003: 76)

From this perspective it may be true that SF is a metaphorical mode, but then so is everything else, so that doesn't help us very much. Perhaps a way out of the bind is to distinguish between 'dead metaphors' and 'vital' ones, a distinction that is implied in Suvin's discussion. Talking about 'the sunrise' does not make the concept new to us (as Aristotle said metaphor should), but talking of life as a virtual-reality prison perhaps does. But I don't think this will do: Dickens' *Little Dorrit* (1855–7) also imagines life metaphorically as a prison, and yet its tenor and impact are quite different from the *Matrix* movies. Even 'vital' metaphors limit the eloquence of a text to a one-to-one estrangement, and 'vital' metaphors are equally ubiquitous in non-SF as in SF.

Other critics bring in the notion of 'metonymy' (also called 'synecdoche') in tandem with metaphor to address this question. Metaphor is talking about something in terms of something else ('bread is the staff of life'); metonymy is talking about some part of an object as if it represents the whole thing ('one hundred head of cattle', 'a parish of two thousand souls'). Following the linguist Roman Jakobson, many critics have taken 'metaphor' and 'metonymy' to be the twin axes of signification, one 'vertical' the other 'horizontal' – although those two terms are, of course, in turn metaphorical. Roger Luckhurst efficiently summarises this position, invoking two of the giants of SF criticism as illustration, Suvin and Samuel Delany:

> An opposition initially formulated by Roman Jakobson, metaphor operates by the *selection* of terms in a tension of dis/similarity, whilst metonymy works by the *combination* of terms in a contiguous, syntagmatic proximity. Jakobson tended to distribute poetry to metaphor and prose to metonymy; science fiction, it is clear, can be located on either pole. So, for Suvin, 'it should be made clear that the sf universe of discourse presents ... possible worlds as ... totalising and thematic metaphors', whilst for Delany the focus is on 'the most basic level of sentence meaning [where] we read words differently when we read them as science fiction'. Suvin, in other words, isolates the specificity of science fiction in the rigour of its cognitive leap between levels (metaphor), whereas Delany insists that the conjunctions and disjunctions of science fiction be located in the science fictional sentence (metonymy).
>
> (Luckhurst 2000: 70)

But Delany does not stress the 'similarities' between the SF-world and the world we all inhabit. In fact, rather the reverse is the case; he stresses the *surplus* of metaphor, and identifies exactly this surplus as the imaginative motor behind the genre.

> A metaphor (or simile) always produces a logical structure – a structure that, in itself, is almost always wholly semantic. (Why is a raven like a writing desk? Because Poe wrote on both.) But there's always a psychological surplus, poetic and organised far more at the level of the letter (Feathers, leather, wings, wood, stone, bone, beak, brass, eyes, handles, claws, drawers ...) and the tension between the logical semantic structure and the psychological, poetic surplus is, I think, what produces the energy and vividness of metaphor.
>
> (Delany 1994: 174)

Delany is surely quite right that SF works *because* of this surplus; it is the infusoria of detail, the minutiae of starship-design, characters, imagined backstories (filled in by fan fiction), social structures, alien biology, timelines, religions, languages and so on that give *Star Trek* or *Dune* their heft, their purchase upon the minds of fans, and not any supposedly core 'metaphorical' meaning in the texts. Indeed, to suggest that these two texts are in effect saying 'humanity is a rainbow coalition that can overcome any obstacle' and 'life is a mysterious desert infested with monsters that can nevertheless produce marvels' is to give some sense of how reductive this manner of analysis is.

I think what this means is that a thoroughgoing analysis of SF-as-metonymy would collapse almost as soon as it began. Asimov's robots, Herbert's sandworms, Wells's invisible heatray, these things do not function metonymically, except in the facile sense that everything is a part of the whole that is the cosmos, and SF does not, of course, operate in this sense. But it may be that we can talk of SF as a metaphoric literature with an understanding that the focus of any SF text is on the 'poetic surplus' rather than the semantic content of the metaphor.

METAPHOR AND THE LITERAL

For some critics the purchase provided by SF depends upon a certain interrelation between literal and metaphorical readings of the text's specifics. Rosemary Jackson's study of non-realist literature *Fantasy: the Literature of Subversion* (1981) insists that 'when it is "naturalised" as allegory or symbolism, fantasy loses its proper non-signifying nature' precisely because 'part of its power lies in this resistance to allegory and metaphor' (Jackson 1981: 41). According to Jackson's reading, Fantasy, and by implication SF, 'takes metaphorical constructions literally'.

Is this right? In part, Jackson's argument that 'fantasy is not metaphorical' depends upon her belief that science fiction or Fantasy 'does not create images which are "poetic" ', but rather 'produces a sliding of one form into another, in a metonymical displacement' (Jackson 1981: 82). Other critics have located SF in a slippage between metaphor and literality: 'language is not trustworthy in sf,' suggests Farah Mendlesohn, 'metaphor becomes literal. "He gave her his hand" or "he turned on his side" raise numerous possibilities in the mind of the sf reader, involving, perhaps, detachable body parts or implanted electronics' (James and Mendlesohn 2003: 5).

To revisit the short list of metaphors I instanced at the beginning of this chapter:

- Juliet is the sun
- Eric Clapton is God
- Day-to-day life is a virtual-reality prison constructed by machine-intelligences.

When watching *Romeo and Juliet* no reasonable person (to slip into the jargon of British law courts) would literally believe Romeo's assertion that Juliet is the sun; if she were literally the sun, then she would consume the entirety of Verona in nuclear fire. Here everybody understands that the language is being used in a figurative and not literal sense.

The Eric Clapton example is more complex. Whilst few people might believe that guitarist Clapton *literally* partakes of divinity, there have been many examples in human culture where groups of people have taken human beings to be divine in a literal, rather than (or as well as) a metaphorical sense. The divinity of Christ or Krishna is, for many, literal, and it is conceivable, if not actual, that a church of Elvis Presley, or John Lennon, or Kurt Cobain, or even of Eric Clapton might one day be established. To say this is only to say that history testifies to the fact that human beings will worship almost anything and almost anybody, depending on the circumstances.

Which in turn is to say that religion is one discourse that elides literal and metaphorical interpretation. Science fiction is another; the statement 'day-to-day life is a virtual-reality prison constructed by machine-intelligences', referencing the *Matrix* movies, seems to me a metaphor; but it has been taken by some as a literal reality. For instance, that is the argument taken by Jake Horsley's book *Matrix Warrior* (Gollancz, 2002).

This suggests the notion that SF is a discursive space that enables the wish-fulfilment to span this gap between metaphoric and literal. Perhaps we, as readers, love the way our favourite writers have represented imaginary spaces, Oz or Middle Earth or wherever. Perhaps, for some, this love is so deep that their wish to literalise and visit these locations becomes overwhelming. In life this is not possible. SF, however, is crammed with devices that make this possible, as with Heinlein's *The Number of the Beast* (1980), in which pushing a gyroscope from three directions at once opens (bizarrely) a vast number of inter-cosmic gateways that in turn enable the novel's protagonists to travel to alternate realities, amongst which are literalised versions of Oz, Barsoom and Heinlein's own fictions (although not Middle Earth).

Much SF is premised on exactly this reading-the-metaphor-as-literal. Farmer's *Riverworld* series literally brings back to life historical and fictional characters. C. J. Cherryh's *Port Eternity* concerns androids who have been constructed and programmed to reproduce the world of King Arthur and his Knights for a wealthy spacefaring woman; or ... examples multiply. *Star Trek*'s 'holodeck' enables people to wander through literalisations of any number of imaginary worlds; myriad SF versions of 'cyberspace' or 'VR' enable the same thing. In Alan Moore's graphic novel *The League of Extraordinary Gentlemen* every imaginative creation of the nineteenth century is literalised; in this text vampires are not merely metaphors for life-draining people such as capitalist overlords, sexually possessive women and so on; they are literally real. We might ask: why is there this crotchet in SF, this urge to literalise the metaphor?

One difficulty with thinking of SF as metaphor is that the second term in metaphor is already presupposed to be not actual. When Romeo says 'Juliet is the sun', we immediately downgrade the second term (she's not actually a sun) in a way we don't with the first term (since she is actually Juliet). A pedant might point out that Juliet is an imaginary character, played by an actress, in just the same way that the rhetorical 'sun' is an imaginary quantity invoked by the poet, but the truth of the experience of watching *Romeo and Juliet* is that because we care about Juliet, we relate to her as if she were real, whereas we relate to the metaphorical comparison of Juliet to the sun as a rhetorical device. To put this another way: the statement 'Juliet is the sun' involves a term we prioritise, take as real (Juliet), and a term we deprioritise, take as fictive (sun).

Extrapolate this to a whole genre, and the implication is as follows: to call SF a metaphoric genre is to place all the imaginative constructions of SF in inferior relation to reality. We believe in real life, but, however illuminating and fertile the idea may be, we don't believe that real life is actually a virtual-reality program set up by malign machine-intelligences to turn us into slaves.

In other words, reading SF as metaphor tends to denigrate SF; it turns a work like Alan Moore and Dave Gibbons' graphic novel *Watchmen* into an egregiously fictive thought-experiment, a bloodless mental elaboration of the question 'what if superheroes were real?'. But this is not the case. *Watchmen* is not a dispassionate thought-experiment; it is a vivid and wholly engrossing textual world, a narrative into which the reader is fully and unembarrassedly drawn, certainly as real as the world of office politics and polite conversations with neighbours one hardly knows.

Moreover, Heinlein's *Number of the Beast*, predicated upon the literalisation of the metaphoric worlds of SF, is a cardboard exercise by an exhausted SF imagination. *Watchmen*, predicated upon the tacit acceptance of the metaphoric world presented, is a deeply involving and moving experience. SF at its best engages us wholly. This is more than a second-hand metaphoricity, removed and subordinate to the literal. It is even more than a Suvinian metaphoricity leavened with 'coherence and richness'. There needs to be some other sense of metaphor that we can use.

RICOEUR

The thinker who most thoroughly explored metaphor in the twentieth century is the French philosopher Paul Ricoeur. His enormous study of 1975, *The Rule of Metaphor*, excavates and revivifies the study of metaphor, opposing the negative cast of Nietzsche's, and Derrida's, scorn for 'dead metaphors' with a valorisation of the positive force metaphor exercises in compelling thought. The French title of the study (poorly served by its common English translation) makes his opposition to Nietzsche plain: *La metaphore vive*. For Ricoeur metaphor is indeed alive; dead metaphors such as 'sunrise' are, he argues, relatively trivial. Living metaphors, which compel us to think more, are much more crucial to language and thought. For Ricoeur metaphor opens new possibilities; it is an imaginative and creative act.

SF is imaginative literature, but so is all literature. Is it true to say that SF can 'force conceptual thought to think more' than other literatures? Or do the heaps of dead-metaphorical spaceships, robots, rayguns, hyperspace-portals, sexy alien women, sentient planets and so on deaden and diminish the power of the medium? How many living metaphors are there in SF?

Metaphor involves not only a simple translation from noun to noun, but, as Delany says, a surplus. Ricoeur points out that the metaphorical statement 'man is a wolf' does more than simply translate man into wolf; which is to say, the word wolf here 'operates not on the basis of its current lexical meaning', but rather invokes 'the opinions and preconceptions to which a reader in a linguistic community ... finds himself committed' (Ricoeur 2003: 101). Indeed, it does more than this, because 'the system of implications does not remain unchanged by the action of the metaphorical utterance'.

> To apply the system is to contribute at the same time to its determination – the wolf appears more human at the same moment that by calling the man a wolf one places the man in a special light.
>
> (Ricoeur 2003: 102)

In other words, the relationship between metaphorical and literal is a dialectical one, mutually self-determining. He pinpoints the 'inescapably paradoxical character surrounding a metaphorical concept of truth':

> The paradox consists in the fact that there is no other way to do justice to the metaphorical notion of truth than to include the critical incision of the (literal) 'is not' within the ontological vehemence of the (metaphorical) 'is' ... it is this tensional constitution of the verb *to be* that receives its grammatical mark in the 'to be like' of metaphor elaborated into simile, at the same time as the tension between *same* and *other* is marked in the relational copula.
>
> (Ricoeur 2003: 302)

Karl Simms' lucid explanation is useful here as a gloss on Ricoeur:

> Arriving at metaphorical truth is not a question of judgment on the reader's part. If it were, we would either have to choose between Achilles being a lion or his not being a lion, which would take away the point of the metaphor, or we would have to accept a contradiction (Achilles both is and is not a lion), which would be silly. Rather, arriving at metaphorical truth is a question of the reader suspending, or bracketing off, their judgment regarding the literal truth of the proposition. Understanding metaphor is a phenomenology of reading.
>
> (Simms 2003: 75)

This, I think, is coming closer to the way SF actually works. Most of us do not believe in the Matrix, or Barsoom, in a facile literalist way, but nor do we denigrate their existence as 'merely' metaphorical, less than real.

Ricoeur's theory of metaphor is part of his broader philosophy of 'hermeneutics', his enquiry into the business of interpreting the world in which we live. In his 1967 study *The Symbolism of Evil* he explores the way *semantic* (or literal) and *symbolic* (or metaphorical) readings interrelate. The statement 'two plus two equals four' is literally true. On a semantic level it always has been and always will be true, whether there are humans around to verify it or not. But the symbolic significance of this statement depends upon human interpretation; in Orwell's *Nineteen Eighty-four*, for example, O'Brien tortures Smith until he accepts that

$2 + 2 = 5$ by way of breaking his will and conditioning him to 'love Big Brother'. In this case, the statement $2 + 2 = 4$ has a range of symbolic meanings, to do with individual freedom and resistance.

To talk of symbols rather than metaphors is, perhaps, a more fruitful way of apprehending the 'point of difference' that defines SF. It aligns SF with poetry, which is where it surely belongs, rather than science, and it expresses the complex of interpretive relations between 'poetry' and 'speculative thought'.

First, the poetry. One of the arguments I make in this book is that SF, as a symbolist discourse, is akin to poetry. I could go further here and suggest that the key moments in the SF of the last half century are in essence poetic moments; the resonance and mystery as well as the beauty of a poetic image is what makes luminous (as it might be) the ape throwing its bone into the sky to metamorphose into a spacecraft; or the star-drenched sky of the final paragraph of *Nightfall*; or Wyndham's unsettling Midwich children; or Carrie-Anne Moss suspended in mid-air kung-fu as the camera sweeps all the way around her; or the eerie silences of the first two books of Robinson's *Years of Rice and Salt*. There are many hundreds of examples from the best SF, and they all work precisely as poetic images work.

Second, the aspect of speculative thought. It is this, I suppose, that most readers of SF come to the genre for. Extrapolation, the imaginative inhabitation of new possibilities, gives SF vigour and power. But, reading via Ricoeur, these two aspects, poetry and speculative thought, are precisely the two dialectical arms of living metaphor.

> On the one hand, poetry, in itself and by itself, sketches a 'tensional' conception of truth for thought. Here are summed up all the forms of 'tensions' brought to light by semantics: tension between subject and predicate, between literal interpretation and metaphorical interpretation, between identity and difference ... they come to completion, finally, in the paradox of the copula, where being-as signifies being and not being ...
>
> Speculative thought, on the other hand, bases its work upon the dynamism of metaphorical utterance, which it construes according to its own sphere of meaning. Speculative discourse can respond in this way only because the *distanciation*, which constitutes the critical

> moment, is contemporaneous with the experience of belonging that
> is opened or recovered by poetic discourse, and because poetic dis-
> course ... prefigures the distanciation that speculative thought carries
> to its highest point of reflection.
>
> (Ricoeur 2003: 370)

For our purposes, we can take Ricoeur's 'distanciation' as the imaginative space that opens up between the lives we live in London or Chicago
(or wherever we happen to live) and the lives we live in *Lord of the Rings*
or *Dune*.[1] It is because SF is both poetic and speculative that it is proper
to think of it as metaphoric, in this strong, Ricoeurian way.

In other words, SF *is* metaphorical, but in the strong sense of living
metaphor that Ricoeur outlines, not the weak Aristotelian sense that
lies behind so many critics' usages. This, I think, is what is wrong with
Suvin's detailed analysis; what is missing from his notion of SF as
metaphoric is not 'coherence and richness' (two qualities that are neces-
sities for any great art, surely) but a properly *poetic-speculative* dialectic, a
Ricoeurian sense of metaphor as alive.

RELIGION

The fact that Ricoeur was a committed Christian, and much of his philosophy explores 'the relationship between philosophy and biblical faith'
(Simms 2003: 3), is also crucial, I think. A great deal of SF is fascinated
with religion (see Farah Mendlesohn's excellent article 'Religion and
Science Fiction' for a more detailed discussion – James and Mendlesohn
2003: 264–75), even some SF written by atheists. This might be
because religion is so similar to SF; in some respects religious belief
depends upon an apprehension of the world in which we actually live,
and in some respects it posits a world utterly different from this world.
In other words, we might think of 'religion' as a *metaphore vive* for SF.

Religion is a speculation about the nature of the cosmos that operates symbolically rather than literally. It can never (whatever funda-
mentalists say) be straightforwardly and literally true, but it may
inhabit Ricoeur's 'tensional conception of truth'. What this means, as
far as I can see, is that one way of thinking about SF is as a specifically
non-religious religion, an atheistical theism: SF plays with the ways

the world is not in order to reveal truths about the way the world is. A literalist religion insists that its belief structure is true, but a living-metaphorical religion, a poetic-speculative discourse, opens the paradoxical possibilities of 'is not' and 'is', not in an insistent but rather in a symbolic sense. Its currency is not 'truth' but 'possibility'. This sort of religion is, in a forceful sense, aesthetic, not only in so far that the Bible and the Koran are aesthetic objects as well as religious codes, but also in the sense that speculating about knowledge is inherently aesthetic.

Thomas Docherty makes this point by stressing the vital importance of 'play' to aesthetics. 'Such "play" ', he suggests, 'gives a content to time whilst also giving it a formal sense; it reconciles the particular experience with the more general social-cultural authority.' He quotes from Isobel Armstrong's *The Radical Aesthetic* (2000) to reinforce his point:

> Isobel Armstrong has argued something similar: 'Play, that fundamental activity, is cognate with aesthetic production ... I understand play ... as a form of knowledge itself. Interactive, sensuous, epistemologically charged, play has to do with both the cognitive and the cultural' ... [Play] transforms perception, as when a stick becomes a horse, say, where the stick 'becomes the "pivot" for severing the idea of a horse from the concrete existence of the horse ... Play liberates the child into ideas.'
>
> (Docherty, in Joughin and Malpas 2003: 31)

Docherty goes on:

> The poem is such a pivotal object, releasing its reader into the experiencing of ideas, into thinking as such ... the forming and informing of a self in the spirit of growth, development, and imagining the possibility that the world and its objects might be otherwise than they are. Another word for this, of course, is metaphor; but metaphor as a practice of thought, or, in the words of Ricoeur, as a process of 'cognition, imagination and feeling': in my own terms, a thinking that is always hospitable to otherness.
>
> (Docherty, in Joughin and Malpas 2003: 31)

Here is exactly where we find science fiction, at the point a stick turns into a horse. It might be said that all literature, or all art, does this; but I think that SF is much more playful (in this profound sense) than other literature. It is predicated upon a fundamental *hospitality to otherness*, to the alien, where other aspects of culture compromise. SF is a metaphorical discourse in a particular sense, the cognitive, imaginative, affective, creative sense that Ricoeur opens up. Its metaphor is aesthetic, which is to say poetic and speculative. It is one of the reasons why SF continues to be so splendidly alive.

NOTES

1   Ricoeur takes the term 'distanciation' from the work of Hans-Georg Gadamer, where it is used to describe the way a contemporary reader of an ancient text is made to feel distant from that text, such as is the case when we read Aeschylus or watch Shakespeare and realise that our own culture and assumptions are very different from the culture and assumptions of the authors. My argument is that SF texts contain within themselves an element of distanciation even though the texts are contemporaneously produced, that the narrators of Jack Vance's novels, for instance, embody a sort of instant distanciation. We could explore this idea further; it might explain the appetite for contemporary SF ... fans want works that create this contemporary distanciation and have little time for SF texts that are actually distanciated (like Kepler's *Somnium*).

BIBLIOGRAPHY

BOOKS

Asimov, Isaac [1942; as novel 1951] (1981) *Foundation*, London: Panther.
—— [1954] (1985) *Caves of Steel*, London: Voyager.
—— [1982] (1984) *Foundation's Edge*, London: Voyager.
Banks, Iain M. (1990) *Use of Weapons*, London: Orbit.
Baxter, Stephen (1998) *Titan*, London: Voyager.
Bradley, Marion Zimmer [1965] (1994) *Star of Danger*, New York: Daw.
—— (1978) *Stormqueen*, Bristol: Severn House.
—— [1985] (1993) *The Best of Marion Zimmer Bradley*, ed. Martin H Greenberg, London: Orbit.
Burroughs, Edgar Rice [1912] (1973) *A Princess of Mars*, New York: Del Rey Books.
Butler, Octavia E. [1979] (1988) *Kindred*, London: Women's Press.
—— [1987] (1997) *Dawn*, New York: Warner Books.
—— [1988] (1997) *Adulthood Rites*, New York: Warner Books.
Cherryh, C. J. [1982] (1989) *Port Eternity*, London: VGSF.
Delany, Samuel [1968] (1970) *The Einstein Intersection*, London: Sphere Books.
Dick, Philip K. [1969] (1988) *Ubik*, London: Grafton.
—— [1972] (1984) *Do Androids Dream of Electric Sheep?*, London: Grafton.
Gibson, William [1984] (1993) *Neuromancer*, London: HarperCollins.
Heinlein, Robert [1959] (1998) *Starship Troopers*, London: New English Library.
—— [1961] (1988) *Stranger in a Strange Land*, New York: Ace Books.
—— [1964] (1976) *Farnham's Freehold*, London: New English Library.
Herbert, Frank [1965] (1989) *Dune*, London: New English Library.
—— [1967] (1989) *Dune Messiah*, London: New English Library.
Kepler, Johannes (1634) *[Somnium] Mathematici Olim Imperatorii Somnium. Seu Opus Posthumum De Astronomia Lunari*, ed. M. Ludovico Kepler.
Kessel, John (1989) *Good News from Outer Space*, London: Orb Books.
Le Guin, Ursula [1969] (1991) *The Left Hand of Darkness*, London: Futura.
Lem, Stanislaw [1961; 1971; 1975] (1981) *Solaris; A Perfect Vacuum; The*

Chain of Chance, trans. Joanna Kilmartin, Steve Cox, Louis Iribarne and Michael Kandel, Harmondsworth: Penguin.

McAuley, Paul (1997) *Child of the River: the First Book of Confluence*, London: Victor Gollancz.

—— (1998) *Ancients of Days: the Second Book of Confluence*, London: Orion.

—— (1999) *Shrine of Stars: the Third Book of Confluence*, London: Orion.

McCaffrey, Anne [1969] (1998) *The Ship Who Sang*, London: Corgi.

Meaney, John (1998) *To Hold Infinity*, London: Bantam.

Milton, John [1674] (1993) *Paradise Lost*, ed. Scott Elledge, New York: Norton.

Moorcock, Michael (1974) *The Land Leviathan*, London: Mayflower.

—— (1993) *The Cornelius Quartet*, London: Victor Gollancz.

Robinson, Kim Stanley [1992] (1996) *Red Mars*, London: Voyager.

Russ, Joanna (1972) 'When It Changed', in *Again, Dangerous Visions*, ed. Harlan Ellison, New York: Doubleday.

—— [1975] (1985) *The Female Man*, London: Women's Press.

Shelley, Mary [1818] (1992) *Frankenstein, or the Modern Prometheus*, ed. Maurice Hindle, Harmondsworth: Penguin.

Smith, E. E. 'Doc' [1934] (1997) *Triplanetary*, Epsom: Ripping Publications.

Sorel, Charles [1626] (1909) *La Vraie Histoire Comique de Francion*, ed. Emile Colombey, Paris: Garnier.

Tepper, Sheri [1989] (1996) *Grass*, London: HarperCollins.

Tiptree Jr, James [1973; in book form 1975] (1979) 'The Women Men Don't See', in *Warm Worlds and Otherwise*, New York: Del Rey Books.

Verne, Jules [1864] (2000) *Voyage au centre de la terre*, Paris: Livres de Poche.

Verne, Jules [1865] (2001) *De la terre à la lune*, Paris: Livres de Poche.

Watson, Ian (1975) *The Jonah Kit*, London: VGSF.

Wells, H. G. [1895–1901] (1995) *The Time Machine, The Island of Doctor Moreau, The War of the Worlds, The First Men in the Moon*, in *The Science Fiction, Volume 1*, London: Phoenix.

FILM AND TV

Alien (1979: dir. Ridley Scott)
Aliens (1986: dir. James Cameron)
Alien 3 (1992: dir. David Fincher)
Alien Resurrection (1997: dir. Jean-Pierre Jeunet)

Apollo 13 (1996: dir. Ron Howard)
Blade Runner (1982: dir. Ridley Scott)
Lost in Space (1998: dir. Stephen Hopkins)
Predator (1987: dir. John McTiernan)
Robocop (1987: dir. Paul Verhoeven)
Star Trek (TV episode: 'Let That Be Your Last Battlefield')
Star Trek: the Next Generation (TV episodes: 'The Best of Both Worlds I
    and II'; 'The Masterpiece Society'; 'Darmok at Jilad')
Star Trek 2: the Wrath of Khan (1982: dir. Nicholas Meyer)
Star Trek 3: the Search for Spock (1984: dir. Leonard Nimoy)
Star Trek 4: the Voyage Home (1986: dir. Leonard Nimoy)
Star Wars (1977: dir. George Lucas)
Star Wars: the Empire Strikes Back (1980: dir. Irvin Kerschner)
Star Wars: Return of the Jedi (1983: dir. Richard Marquand)
Star Wars: the Phantom Menace (1999: dir. George Lucas)
Westworld (1973: dir. Michael Crichton)
2001: a Space Odyssey (1968: dir. Stanley Kubrick)

CRITICISM

Abrams, M. H. (1985) *A Glossary of Literary Terms*, 5th edition, Fort
    Worth, TX: Holt, Rinehart and Winston.
Aldiss, Brian [1973] (1986) *Billion Year Spree: the History of Science
    Fiction*, London: Wiedenfeld and Nicolson. Updated in 1986 as
    Trillion Year Spree, London: Gollancz.
Alkon, Paul K. (1994) *Science Fiction before 1900: Imagination Discovers
    Technology*, London: Routledge.
Armitt, Lucie (ed.) (1991) *Where No Man Has Gone Before: Women and
    Science Fiction*, London and New York: Routledge.
Amis, Kingsley (ed.) (1981) *The Golden Age of Science Fiction*,
    Harmondsworth: Penguin.
Barr, Marleen S. (1987) *Alien to Femininity: Speculative Fiction and
    Feminist Theory*, Westport, CT: Greenwood Press.
—— (1993) *Lost in Space: Probing Feminist Science Fiction and Beyond*,
    Chapel Hill: University of North Carolina Press.
Barron, Neil (ed.) (1995) *Anatomy of Wonder: a Critical Guide to Science
    Fiction*, 4th edition, New York: Bowker.
Broderick, Damien (1995) *Reading by Starlight: Postmodern Science
    Fiction*, London and New York: Routledge.
Bukatman, Scott (1993) *Terminal Identity: the Virtual Subject in*

    Postmodern Science Fiction, Durham, NC, and London: Duke University Press.

Clute, John (1995) *Look at the Evidence: Essays and Reviews*, Liverpool: Liverpool University Press.

Clute, John and Peter Nicholls (eds) (1993) *The Encyclopedia of Science Fiction*, London: Orbit.

Csicsery-Ronay Jr, Istvan (1991) 'Science Fiction and Postmodernism', *Science-Fiction Studies* 18:3, 305–8.

Delany, Samuel (1994) *Silent Interviews: on Language, Race, Sex, Science Fiction and Some Comics*, Hanover, PA, and London: Wesleyan University Press.

Dery, Mark (ed.) (1993) 'Flame Wars: the Discourse of Cyberculture', *The South Atlantic Quarterly* 92:4, Fall, 627–45.

Docherty, Thomas (1996) *Alterities: Criticism, History, Representation*, Oxford: Clarendon Press.

—— (2003) 'Aesthetic education and the demise of experience', in John J. Joughin and Simon Malpas (eds) *The New Aestheticism*, Manchester: Manchester University Press, 23–35.

Donawerth, Jane (1997) *Frankenstein's Daughters: Women Writing Science Fiction*, New York: Syracuse University Press.

Donawerth, Jane and Carol A. Kolmerten (eds) (1994) *Utopian and Science Fiction by Women: Worlds of Difference*, Liverpool: Liverpool University Press.

Eshun, Kodwo (1998) *More Brilliant than the Sun: Adventures in Sonic Fiction*, London: Quartet.

Fredericks, Casey (1982) *The Future of Eternity: Mythologies of Science Fiction and Fantasy*, Bloomington: Indiana University Press.

Freedman, Philip (1984) 'Towards a Theory of Paranoia: the Science Fiction of Philip K Dick', *Science-Fiction Studies* 11:2, 15–24.

Gray, Chris Hables, Heidi J. Figuroa-Sarriera and Steven Mentor (eds) (1995) *The Cyborg Handbook*, London: Routledge.

Griffiths, John (1980) *Three Tomorrows: American, British and Soviet Science Fiction*, London: Macmillan.

Harraway, Donna J. (1991) 'A Cyborg Manifesto: Science, Technology, and Social-Feminism in the Late Twentieth Century', in *Simians, Cyborgs and Women: the Reinvention of Nature*, London: Free Association Books.

Harrison, Taylor (1996) 'Weaving the Cyborg Shroud: Mourning and Deferral in *Star Trek: the Next Generation*', in T. Harrison, S. Projanski, K. Ono and E. Helford (eds), *Enterprise Zones: Critical Positions on Star Trek*, Boulder, CO: Westview.

Harvey, John (1995) *Men in Black*, London: Reaktion Books.

Huntington, John (1989) *Rationalising Genius: Ideological Strategies in the Classic American Science Fiction Short Story*, New Brunswick, NJ, and London: Rutgers University Press.

Jackson, Rosemary (1981) *Fantasy: the Literature of Subversion*, London: Routledge.

James, Edward (1994) *Science Fiction in the 20th Century*, Oxford: Oxford University Press.

James, Edward and Farah Mendlesohn (eds) (2003) *The Cambridge Companion to Science Fiction*, Cambridge: Cambridge University Press.

Jameson, Frederic (1984) 'Postmodernism, or the Cultural Logic of Late Capitalism', *New Left Review* 143, 53–94.

—— (1990) *Postmodernism, or the Cultural Logic of Late Capitalism*, London: Verso.

Jenkins, Henry (1992) *Textual Poachers: Television, Fans and Participatory Culture*, London: Routledge.

Jones, Gwyneth (1999) *Deconstructing the Starships: Science, Fiction and Reality*, Liverpool: Liverpool University Press.

Joughin, John J. and Simon Malpas (eds) (2003) *The New Aestheticism*, Manchester: Manchester University Press.

Kristeva, Julia (1982) *Powers of Horror: an Essay in Abjection*, New York: Columbia University Press.

Kuhn, Annette (ed.) (1990) *Alien Zone: Cultural Theory and Contemporary Science Fiction Cinema*, London: Verso.

Le Guin, Ursula (1989) *The Language of the Night: Essays on Fantasy and Science Fiction*, London: Women's Press.

Lefanu, Sarah (1988) *In the Chinks of the World Machine: Feminism and Science Fiction*, London: Women's Press.

Luckhurst, Roger (1997) *'The Angle Between Two Walls': the Fiction of J. G. Ballard*, Liverpool: Liverpool University Press.

—— (1998) 'The Science Fictionalisation of Trauma: Remarks on Narratives of Alien Abduction', *Science-Fiction Studies* 25:1, 1–12.

—— (2000) 'Vicissitudes of the Voice, Speaking Science Fiction', in Andy Sawyer and David Seed (eds) *Speaking Science Fiction: Dialogues and Interpretations*, Liverpool: Liverpool University Press, 69–81.

—— (2005) Science Fiction, London: Polity.

McCracken, Scott (1998) *Pulp: Reading Popular Fiction*, Manchester: Manchester University Press.

Manlove, Colin Nicholas (1986) *Science Fiction: Ten Explorations*, Kent, OH: Kent State University Press.

Marx, Karl [1867] (1976) *Capital*, Vol. 1 (transl. B Foukes), Harmondsworth: Penguin.

Morgan, Chris (1980) *The Shape of Futures Past: the Story of Prediction*, Exeter: Webb and Bower.

Nicholls, Peter (ed.) (1981) *The Encyclopedia of Science Fiction*, London: Granada.

Nietzsche, Friedrich [1873] 'On Truth and Lie in an Extra-Moral Sense', in Walter Kaufmann (ed. and transl.) *The Portable Nietzsche*, New York: Viking Press, 1968, 42–7

O'Reilly, Timothy (1981) *Frank Herbert*, New York: Ungar.

Parkin, Lance (1999) Letter to *Interzone* 139 (January), 4–5.

Parrinder, Patrick (ed.) (1979) *Science Fiction: a Critical Guide*, London: Longman.

—— (1980) *Science Fiction: Its Criticism and Teaching*, London and New York: Methuen.

—— (2000) 'Revisiting Suvin's Poetics of Science Fiction', in P. Parrinder (ed.) *Learning from Other Worlds: Estrangement, Cognition and the Politics of Science Fiction and Utopia*, Liverpool: Liverpool University Press, 36–50

Ricoeur, Paul (2003) *The Rule of Metaphor: the Creation of Meaning in Language*, transl. Robert Czerny, with Kathleen McLaughlin and John Costello, London: Routledge.

Roberts, Robin (1993) *A New Species: Gender and Science in Science Fiction*, Urbana: University of Illinois Press.

Russ, Joanna (1972) 'The Image of Women in Science Fiction', in S. K. Cornillon (ed.) *Images of Women in Fiction*, Bowling Green, KY: Bowling Green University Popular Press.

Scholes, Robert (1975) *Structural Fabulation: an Essay on Fiction of the Future*, Bloomington: Indiana University Press.

Simms, Karl (2003) *Paul Ricoeur*, London: Routledge.

Slusser, George and Tom Shippey (eds) (1992) *Fiction 2000: Cyberpunk and the Future of Narrative*, Athens and London: University of Georgia Press.

Stockwell, Peter (2000) *The Poetics of Science Fiction*, Harlow: Longman.

Suvin, Darko (1979) *Metamorphoses of Science Fiction: on the Poetics and History of a Literary Genre*, New Haven, CT: Yale University Press.

—— (1988) *Positions and Presuppositions in Science Fiction*, London: Macmillan.

Tulloch, John and Henry Jenkins (1995) *Science Fiction Audiences*, London: Routledge.

Westfahl, Gary (1998) *The Mechanics of Wonder: the Creation of the Idea of Science Fiction*, Liverpool: Liverpool University Press.

—— (1999) 'Janeways and Thaneways; the Better Half, and Worse Half, of Science Fiction Television', *Interzone* 140 (February), 31–3.

Wolmark, Jenny (1994) *Aliens and Others: Science Fiction, Feminism and Postmodernism*, New York and London: Harvester.

INDEX